North East England

Heritage Walks

Compiled by
Dennis and Jan Kelsall

Contents

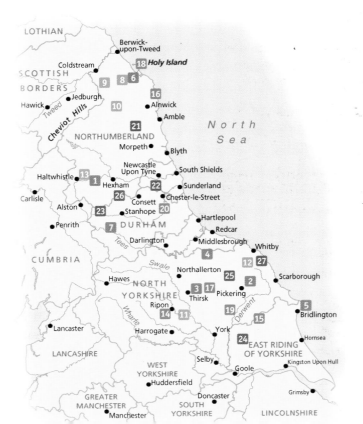

At-a-glance

1 Allen Banks

Rough woodland paths and steep ground

 3½ miles (5.6km)

 2 hours

2 The Bride Stones

Wood and moorland paths, short climbs

 4½ miles (7.2km)

 2½ hours

3 Sutton Bank

Woodland paths and tracks, steep climbs

 8 miles (12.9km)

4½ hours

4 Roseberry Topping

Wood and moorland paths, steep ground

 6½ miles (10.5km)

4 hours

5 Flamborough Head

Field and cliff paths, short climbs

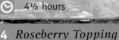 7 miles (11.3km)

4 hours

6 St Cuthbert's Cave

Generally clear tracks and field paths

 7 miles (11.3km)

 4 hours

7 High & Low Force

Generally clear tracks and field paths

 8½ miles (13.7km)

4½ hours

The path by the Bride Stones

Natural Features

Sutton Bank's cliffs reveal 60 million years of geological history

Despite the unremitting sprawl of urbanisation, much of Britain remains rural and even wild, displaying a remarkable diversity and beauty. This is particularly true of the area east of the Pennine watershed between the Tweed and Humber, where the only major conurbations are concentrated upon the mouths of the Tyne, Tees and Humber. Within or straddling its borders are three National Parks, four AONBs and innumerable SSSIs and nature reserves; a landscape that encompasses upland moor, pastoral wold and vale, craggy coastline and forest expanse. The highlighted features reveal the varied facets of the immense natural richness of this countryside and will undoubtedly whet an appetite for further exploration.

Woodlands such as those at **Allen Banks** might appear natural, but in truth have been managed over centuries for timber. The steep-sided gorge precluded farming, but mining, quarrying and lime burning were all once industries. The fast-flowing stream powered mills and in the 14th century, a pele tower offered protection against Scottish raiding parties. Yet none of this compromised its innate beauty and in the 19th century,

'wilderness' walks were laid out to take advantage of the finest views.

The Bride Stones lie at the edge of Dalby Forest, one of many managed by the Forestry Commission, which was created in 1919 to restore and manage the country's timber reserves. With changing policies, recent decades have seen emphasis on amenity planting, which is both aesthetically pleasing and attracts wildlife, and the development of forest trails, camping and even 'Go Ape' to extend recreational usage. The stones themselves outcrop on the spine of a ridge overlooking a secluded valley and are a wonderful illustration of nature's artistic creation.

Sutton Bank forms part of the long escarpment defining the western edge of the North York Moors plateau, a 450-foot cliff of layered sandstone, limestone, shale and mudstone that reveals some 60 million years of geological history. The vertical cliff was scoured during the last ice age by a vast glacier flowing through what is now the Vale of York. It left behind moraines trapping a succession of small lakes along the cliff base, all but Gormire having subsequently drained away. A folk tale, however, attributes its formation to the devil on a galloping horse, which plunged over the cliff leaving a bottomless crater. Kilburn's white horse is a conspicuous example of open-air art rooted in prehistory and more usually found on southern England's chalk downs. Such figures soon disappear without regular maintenance and thus few are of any antiquity.

One of the most distinctive topographical features of the North York Moors, **Roseberry Topping** is a striking hill separated from the main body of the adjoining moorland plateau by a low saddle. What could be more natural? Yet even here, man might have had a hand in shaping its profile. Until 1912 it had an almost perfect 'sugar loaf' profile, but then one night in August a dramatic landslip occurred, truncating its western face into a cliff. It has been suggested that centuries of mining the hill for alum and iron might have exacerbated an existing fault line, precipitating the collapse.

The tip of a promontory projecting into the North Sea, **Flamborough Head** is part of the highest run of cliffs along the English east coast. It is the abrupt culmination of the chalk uplands of the Yorkshire Wolds, laid down in a tropical sea when dinosaurs roamed the earth. Wave erosion has created caves and spectacular stacks, while countless ledges on the towering cliffs attract over 200,000 seabirds to nest each year. Amongst them are razorbill, puffin, guillemot and shag, but by far the most numerous are kittiwake. The cliffs are also home to Britain's largest mainland population of gannets.

Steeped in the legend of a 7th-century Celtic saint, **St Cuthbert's Cave** is a sweeping, shallow cave or rock shelter beneath an overhanging sandstone cliff that gazes out across the valley of the River Till towards the Cheviot Hills. Reputedly a resting-place for Lindisfarne monks fleeing from invading Vikings with their saint's revered body, it is a serenely beautiful spot. The hilltop above commands a superb panorama across the Northumbrian countryside, while out to the east beyond the coast are the Farne islands, where Cuthbert spent the latter part of his life as a hermit.

From its source on the eastern slopes of Cross Fell, the meandering River Tees gathers water from the Pennine moors before thundering from the uplands into a deep ravine. Its upper waterfall is Cauldron Snout below the Cow Green Reservoir, but more accessible and equally dramatic are **High and Low Force**. The falls cascade over great dolerite ledges, part of the Great Whin Sill volcanic intrusion that outcrops dramatically throughout Northumberland and the northern Pennines. Although the dolerite is hard, undercutting of the softer sandstone and limestone upon which it rests causes periodic collapse and, over time, the waterfall retreats upstream leaving behind a deep and narrow gorge. Although not the highest falls in the country, they are truly spectacular and are the largest in terms of water volume.

walk 1

Allen Banks

Start
Allen Banks, near Bardon Mill

Distance
3½ miles (5.6km)

Height gain
770 feet (235m)

Approximate time
2 hours

Route terrain
Rough woodland paths and steep ground

Parking
National Trust car park at start

OS maps
Landranger 86 (Haltwhistle & Brampton) or 87 (Hexham & Haltwhistle), Explorer OL43 (Hadrian's Wall – Haltwhistle & Hexham)

GPS waypoints
🐾 NY 798 639
Ⓐ NY 798 632
Ⓑ NY 794 625
Ⓒ NY 794 622
Ⓓ NY 798 632

Given to the National Trust in 1942 by Francis Bowes Lyon, uncle to the Queen Mother, the beautiful deep, wooded gorge of the River Allen contains some of the largest stands of ancient semi-natural woodland in Northumberland. But few places in this country are truly wild and the secluded valley has been managed for centuries to produce fuel, timber poles and bark for tanning. Explored here is the northern section, where paths and a small lake were laid out during the 19th century to create 'wilderness walks', with small summerhouses constructed to exploit the most dramatic viewpoints. The species-rich woodland supports a wide range of wildlife, and if you go quietly beside the river, you might even spot an otter.

🐾 Follow a path through the picnic area beside the river into the wood. Beyond a suspension bridge, climb to a higher path Ⓐ. Cross and continue the upward trend, slanting more steeply across the wooded bank and eventually zigzagging up the final stretch. Broaching the top, walk on to a reconstruction of the Cedar Wood summerhouse, which contains a 'book' portraying the estate's history.

Bear right on a level path along the rim of the valley, the ride bordered by splendid beech trees that are at their best when the leaves turn in autumn. After a while, the path leads to the site of another summerhouse, perched above the deep ravine of Hoods Burn that falls into the main valley. Although the structure is long gone, the mosaic floor remains, fashioned from the bones of sheep and deer.

An orange waymark indicates the way dropping left. Partly stepped, it is steep and demands care during wet weather.

Looking from the summerhouse into the gorge

Rejoining the main riverside trail **B**, follow it over a plank bridge spanning Hoods Burn. After a small meadow, the path delves into the Briarwood Banks Nature Reserve, an ancient woodland of oak, ash and hazel coppice. Keep left at a fork crossing a side stream to a robust bridge spanning the River Allen **C**. It replaces a suspension bridge that was washed away during a flood in 2005.

Beyond the bridge, bear right to a field gate at Plankey Mill. Swing left in front of a barn to climb away on a narrow lane. As the lane then bends, abandon it for a descending track, keeping left again when that splits to pass a ruined building. Just before it finishes, slip through a kissing-gate on the left from which a contained path runs beside a meadow. At the end, drop to continue along the riverbank.

Over a stile and footbridge, the path follows the river into a gorge, picking a rising course amongst a litter of boulders. Ignore an unsigned path off right but as the way then levels, watch for a fork. A black waymark guides you right, climbing above the river. When you later reach another junction, keep ahead to find a purple waymarked path branching up steps, a few yards farther along on the right **D**.

Cresting a rise, it falls to a crossing path where The Tarn is signed to the right. Resume the climb to another crossing and this time go left up steps. There is a view across the River South Tyne Valley before, a little lower down, The Tarn suddenly appears in front of you. Surrounded by trees, it occupies an idyllically picturesque spot.

Joining a broader path, pass left of the pool. At the far end, look out for another purple waypost from which a narrow path bears left. Over a low rise, it doubles back in easy descent across the wooded slope of the hill, eventually returning you to the crossing passed on the way up.

Still following purple waymarks, turn right. At the next junction, go left and then left again to come upon the steps by which you began the ascent to The Tarn. Now swing sharp right, losing height steeply to meet the River Allen at a suspension bridge. You can either cross and retrace your outward route or alternatively, continue downstream on this bank. Leaving the wood carry on at the edge of a couple of meadows, ultimately approaching a bridge. Walk beneath it and then turn up to the lane, which leads across the river back to the car park. ●

SCALE 1:25000 or 2½ INCHES to 1 MILE 4CM to 1KM

ALLEN BANKS ● 9

The Bride Stones

Start

Low Staindale (reached along Dalby Forest Drive - toll)

Distance

4½ miles (7.2km)

Height gain

520 feet (160m)

Approximate time

2½ hours

Route terrain

Wood and moorland paths, short climbs

Parking

Car park at start

OS maps

Landrangers 94 (Whitby & Esk Dale) and 101 (Scarborough), Explorer OL27 (North York Moors – Eastern area)

GPS waypoints

SE 877 904
Ⓐ SE 874 913
Ⓑ SE 873 924
Ⓒ SE 867 912
Ⓓ SE 861 908

The Bride Stones outcrop spectacularly at the edge of the moor above a small, secluded valley that is a wonderful haven for all manner of wildlife. The rocks, weathered into weird and wonderful shapes by wind, rain and frost, are of fine sandstone, whose colour adds another dimension to their intriguing beauty.

A path across grass behind the north side of the car park leads past a National Trust marker to a gate and kissing-gate. Ignore them and go right, but take the left fork just beyond, climbing the oak-clad hillside of Low Wood. At the top, bear right through birch trees onto open moorland, making for the Low Bride Stones.

Continue beyond the last of the craggy outcrops to a point where the path bends left Ⓐ. To reach the High Bride Stones, carry on down across Bridestone Griff and then turn right.

Return to point Ⓐ and now climb steeply to the left along a narrow track through the heather. At the top of the bank, go left along a well-trodden moorland trail above the head of Bridestone Griff to meet a grass track. Follow that left beside an area of regenerating forest for ½ mile until you reach the edge of the moor Ⓑ. Turn left along an uneven path, keeping a fence on your right. After passing a pond, negotiate a patch of rough,

The striking stones

The striking stones lie in two groups along the top of parallel ridges, their name probably derived from a Norse word meaning 'brink' or 'edge' stones, although an alternative theory suggests they may have been the focus of an ancient fertility ceremony. But folklore offers a more romantic explanation; crossing the moor after their wedding a young couple was suddenly engulfed in mist and sought temporary refuge amongst the rocks.

Such formations are not unique and can occur where sandstone outcrops have been exposed to the elements. Sandstone is a sedimentary rock, and was laid down here in tropical seas during the Jurassic period some 150 million years ago. Changing conditions during its formation created strata, not only with different colours, but also varying degrees of hardness, which has resulted in each layer weathering at its own rate to create bizarre and fantastic shapes.

marshy grass and then climb a stile. Turn left along a farm track across Grime Moor, where shortly, the Bride Stones come back into view.

Eventually, pass through a gate to a junction by High Pastures Farm **C**. Turn through another gate on the right and walk out to follow a fence on the left. Where the ground then begins to fall, swing through a gap on the left and walk along the top edge of a narrowing enclosure. Towards the far end veer away, dropping to a stile in the bottom far corner. Climb diagonally across the middle of the next field, turning left along its top edge to emerge through a gate onto a lane **D**.

Follow it left into a dip, but then take a waymarked track on the left just beyond. Keep ahead through a yard at Low Pasture Farm, leaving along a track, signed to the Bride Stones, which descends through fields and into woodland. Over a stile, carry on down and then around a bend by a cottage. Go left past its front, rising to walk away along a grassy path, which later drops to cross a

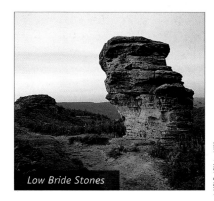

Low Bride Stones

stream. Continue by a fence along the bottom edge of Low Wood to a kissing-gate and on back to the car park. ●

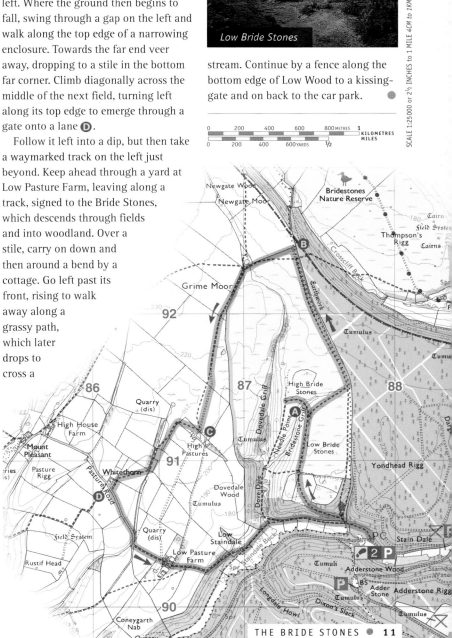

Sutton Bank

Start

Sutton Bank National Park Information Centre and café

Distance

8 miles (12.9km)

Height gain

1,450 feet (440m)

Approximate time

4½ hours

Route terrain

Woodland paths and tracks, steep climbs

Parking

Car park at start

OS maps

Landranger 100 (Malton & Pickering), Explorer OL26 (North York Moors – Western area)

GPS waypoints

SE 516 830
Ⓐ SE 514 811
Ⓑ SE 514 806
Ⓒ SE 503 825
Ⓓ SE 508 825
Ⓔ SE 501 843
Ⓕ SE 508 851

The imposing nature of Sutton Bank is revealed right from the start. To the left, the walk runs above the almost vertical cliffs of Roulston Scar, beyond which, but as yet hidden, lies the White Horse of Kilburn. Spread below are the Hood Hill plantations and open fields surrounding Hood Grange Farm, while just north are the silent, tree-fringed waters of Gormire Lake. The return winds above the precipices of Whitestone Cliff and Sutton Brow, which form a dramatic boundary to the rolling Hambleton Hills stretching behind. Tread softly through the woodland and by the lake to see squirrels and perhaps even deer, while the outstanding views from the escarpment across the flat and fertile lands of the Vale of York to the distant Pennines are ample reward for the stiff climb to its airy heights.

From the information centre car park, cross the main road at the top of Sutton Bank to find a path opposite, signed 'Cleveland Way and White Horse'. Where it then forks, bear left past the viewpoint and follow the edge of the escarpment for 1½ miles. After passing a plantation it later runs above Roulston Scar, skirting a small airfield belonging to the Yorkshire Gliding Club to reach the top of the White Horse. After enjoying the superb view south over the Vale of Pickering to the Wolds, turn right down steep steps to a car park at the bottom Ⓐ.

The White Horse The White Horse was the brainchild of a local Victorian schoolmaster, John Hodgson, and his friend Thomas Taylor, who wanted to create a figure similar to those that had impressed them on the chalk downlands of southern England. Hodgson organised his pupils to help mark out the horse in 1857, which is 314 feet long and 228 feet high. However, because the underlying stone is dark-coloured, it had to be painted with lime whitewash to make it visible from afar.

Head down the lane from the car park for just over ½ mile to the bottom of the hill, there turning right along a tarmac track, marked as a bridleway Ⓑ. Where it shortly turns left towards a farm, keep ahead on a gravel path that soon rises steadily through a plantation, eventually meeting a broad forestry track. Now go left and follow it down to a major fork, there bearing left again. As you climb away, there is an impressive view of the sheer cliffs of Roulston Scar towering above the trees, an indication of just how far you have descended. Some ¼ mile farther along as the track curves left, leave at the end of the trees on the right by a sign to Hood Grange and the A170. Emerging at the edge of an open field, follow a clear path ahead towards Hood Grange Farm. At the far side, turn beside a brook in front of the farm to a footbridge and walk up at the edge of a small paddock to a track at the top. Cross a ladder-stile almost opposite and continue straight up the fields in front to a stile in the top hedge adjoining the main road **C**.

Follow the road verge to the right for some 600 yds, before turning off left through a gate **D**. Marked as a bridleway, the track climbs to Gormire Farm. Keep ahead past the farm and through a gate to a junction by Gormire Lake.

Bear right on a wooded path signed to Southwoods around its eastern shore, eventually reaching a junction well beyond the head of the lake. Joining a

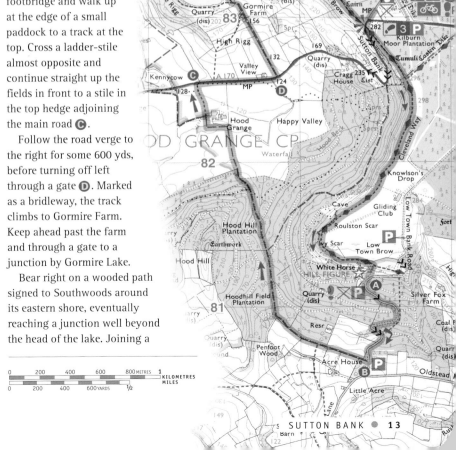

SCALE 1:25000 or 2½ INCHES to 1 MILE 4CM to 1KM

```
0      200    400    600    800 METRES   1
                                          KILOMETRES
                                          MILES
0      200    400    600 YARDS    ½
```

bridleway from Thirlby Bank, carry on a little farther to emerge from the trees opposite Southwoods Lodge.

Turn right through a gate and carry on along a bridleway that eventually meets a crossing of tracks at the entrance to Southwoods Hall **E**. Signed to Tang Hall and Southwoods, the way continues beside the hedge through a wooden gate opposite. At a second gate, slip through to join the drive, but where that then bends left towards the hall,

Gormire Lake

Despite its proximity to a main road and a well-frequented walking-area, the lake has a decidedly remote and mysterious atmosphere. It occupies a hollow in the debris of a glacial moraine and is unusual in that the pool has neither inlet nor outlet, its level entirely regulated by underground drainage.

keep ahead to a field gate.

Instead of passing through, follow the fence to the right below barns to a small gate. Crossing a stream, bear left up the edge of a field. At the corner of the wall, a sign indicating the Cleveland Way directs you right to a waypost a few yards away. Swing left up the bank and continue uphill, the ongoing path confirmed by occasional blue-topped markers. Through a gate bear left, rising quite steeply to another gate leading into a forestry plantation. Carry on upwards through the trees, shortly reaching a grassy track. Walk a few paces to the right and then turn sharp left to resume your ascent. Emerging from the forest, head left in a final short pull onto the Cleveland Way **F**. Turn right for an exhilarating but easy ramble of nearly two miles along the top of the scarp back to Sutton Bank, enjoying magnificent views all the way. ●

The reedy banks of Gormire Lake

Roseberry Topping

Start
Gribdale Gate,
2½ miles east of
Great Ayton

Distance
6½ miles (10.5km)

Height gain
1,320 feet (400m)

Approximate time
4 hours

Route terrain
Wood and moorland
paths, steep ground

Parking
Car park at start

OS maps
Landranger 93
(Middlesbrough),
Explorer OL26 (North
York Moors - Western
area)

GPS waypoints
NZ 591 110
Ⓐ NZ 589 101
Ⓑ NZ 577 109
Ⓒ NZ 563 107
Ⓓ NZ 578 126

To the east of Great Ayton lie two of the most prominent land-marks of the Cleveland Hills: the 19th-century monument to Captain Cook on Easby Moor and the dramatic 1,051 feet hill, Roseberry Topping, whose distinctive silhouette is visible from many vantage points on the moor as well as the plain below.

From the car park go through a gate into the Cleveland Forest and follow a broad track, the Cleveland Way, signed towards Kildale. The way climbs easily for ½ mile, eventually emerging on to Easby Moor. Keep straight ahead to the Cook Monument Ⓐ.

> **The Cook Monument** It was erected in 1827 to commemorate the extraordinary achievements of Captain James Cook. Born into a local farming family, he attended the nearby school in Great Ayton and must have spent many hours during his childhood amongst these hills. Joining the Navy, he became a skilled navigator and cartographer, and the voyages of exploration under the bold and inquisitive spirit of his leadership not only filled in many of the blanks on the map, but also contributed much to the wider knowledge of the world. Rising above the edge of the escarpment, the obelisk commands a panoramic view over the surrounding countryside; the wide sweep of the Cleveland plain below bounded by the distant conurbation of Teesside to the north. Yet it is the sharp profile of Roseberry Topping in the middle distance that grabs the attention, drawing you on to the next leg of the route.

At the monument, turn sharp right along a narrower path across the heather to pass through an ungated gap in a stone wall. Carry on beside a broken boundary, bearing left where it ends at a waymarked fork. Keep right where the path again splits a few paces farther on, slanting from the open heath into Ayton Banks Wood. The clear path falls quite steeply through the trees to meet a broader track near the bottom. Cross and continue downhill a short distance to leave the forest through a gap in the bottom wall. Head down a grassy slope to a track below and go right. Beyond a couple of gates, the way continues as a pleasant sunken path, later broadening to a track

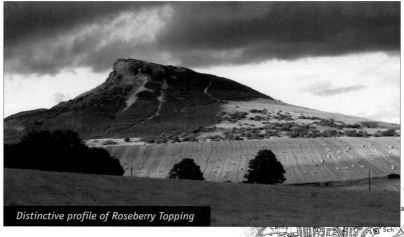

Distinctive profile of Roseberry Topping

and then a metalled lane. Keep going to reach a crossroads with Dikes Lane **B**.

Turn left down the hill, passing the railway station and eventually reaching a roundabout junction. Go right to another junction at the edge of Great Ayton **C**. The heart of the village lies to the left where you will find a museum in the old schoolhouse as well as a number of inviting opportunities for refreshment. The onward route, however, follows Newton Road to the right, leaving about 100 yds along through a kissing-gate breaking the high wall on the right. Pass through a belt of trees and on at the edge of a meadow to a thicket at the far side. A gated path continues across the fields below Cleveland Lodge, largely hidden by its woodland garden, before reaching the railway line.

Exercise care as you cross to a track beyond. Ignore a drive and carry on over a stile opposite to follow the field edge away, ascending towards a tree-lined hillside. At the crest of the rise, go over a stile beside a gate into Cliff Ridge Wood and climb to a broad path above. Diagonally opposite, a path rises to the right across a wooded slope, which is carpeted with bluebells in spring, and emerges into a field at the top. Go left to a stile in the corner and then turn right past a clump of larch. Over another stile, keep ahead towards a cottage, and then swing left, following the boundary a short distance to a stile beside the second of two gates. The ongoing path now makes straight for Roseberry Topping, the gradient becoming steeper as you get nearer. Reaching the upper

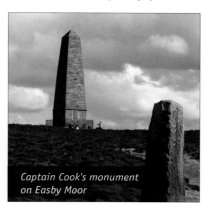

Captain Cook's monument on Easby Moor

Imprints of time

Early prints show that Roseberry Topping once had a perfect conical shape, but subsidence, perhaps caused by tunnelling into the side of the hill for iron ore and alum led to the collapse of the western face, creating the abrupt scar by which it is distinguished today. As might be anticipated, the views from the summit are impressive, a superb panorama that extends to the North Sea coast beyond Guisborough and Teesside. Behind, the Cleveland plain rises abruptly to the moorland hills, the Cook Monument standing as a prominent landmark on the edge above Great Ayton.

SCALE 1:25'000 or 2½ INCHES to 1 MILE 4CM to 1KM

flanks, avoid a direct assault on the summit by curving right to find a zigzag path that leads more easily onto the top **D**.

From the triangulation column, walk back along the crest of the ridge, dropping steeply at the far end to the saddle of Roseberry Common below. Keep ahead, climbing once more beside a wall onto the high ground beyond, where a gate at the top opens onto Newton Moor. As the way then immediately forks, take the right branch, marked with a National Trail symbol. A broad path curves above the hillside plantation for almost 1¼ miles, eventually descending to the lane and parking area at Gribdale Gate. ●

walk 5

Flamborough Head

Start
South Landing,
Flamborough Head

Distance
7 miles (11.3km)

Height gain
960 feet (290m)

Approximate time
4 hours

Route terrain
Field and cliff paths,
short climbs

Parking
Car park at start

OS maps
Landranger 101
(Scarborough),
Explorer 301
(Scarborough,
Bridlington &
Flamborough Head)

GPS waypoints
　　TA 230 695
Ⓐ TA 230 693
Ⓑ TA 253 707
Ⓒ TA 238 719
Ⓓ TA 233 719
Ⓔ TA 231 712
Ⓕ TA 227 705

Flamborough's spectacular chalk cliffs with wave-eroded caves, arches and stacks are a bird watcher's paradise. Each year thousands of seabirds occupy the cliffs, the spectacle at its most impressive between May and July when the adult birds are feeding their broods and the youngsters making their first tentative attempt to fly.

Leaving the car park, follow the wooded lane to South Landing Ⓐ. Just before the lifeboat station, drop left and climb the stepped path onto the headland. Follow it right and then left, shortly reaching a fork by a sculpture representing St Oswald, the patron saint of fishermen.

A fishing past

Like other east-coast villages, Flamborough was a fishing community and, from its two landings, cobble boats once set out to sea, while in early spring, daring young men risked their lives to harvest eggs from the cliffs. More clandestine was smuggling and 'wrecking', the luring of ships onto the rocks for their cargoes.

Take the right branch and carry on along the coast. Glancing back, there is a view to Bridlington, while across the headland are the towers of two generations of lighthouse. Later, ignore a footpath signed towards Lighthouse Road and continue to the tip of Flamborough Head.

Approaching the fog signal station and radio masts, the path forks at a waypost, offering a choice of routes either side of a grassy swathe. Both lead to a track from the signal station. Follow it left towards the lighthouse.

Just before the lighthouse Ⓑ, bear off right onto a path below its seaward wall. Meeting a road, keep right along the cliff top past the car park to a topograph. It shows, amongst other things, that Flamborough Head is equidistant from John o'Groats and Lands End – 362 miles.

Continue along the clifftop path, from which there are dramatic views into the deep bays below, while inland rises a slightly leaning, octagonal chalk tower. It was built in 1669 by Sir John Clayton, and is the oldest light tower to survive in England. However, despite the dangers of this stretch of coast, it was apparently never used for its intended purpose and it was not until the 'new' tower was built in 1806 that a warning light shone from the point.

The path eventually curves in above North Landing, where a track leads down to the beach **C**. Cross and carry on along the seaward edge of the car park, from which the way is signed over a stile to Thornwick Bay. The path immediately drops steeply into a gully, crossing a stream to rise more easily on the opposite side. Walking on, there is a fine picture back into North Landing and then later, the view ahead is of the perpendicular cliffs to the north. Approaching Thornwick, the path winds in above the bay, finally descending a

SCALE 1:27777 or 2¼ INCHES to 1 MILE 3.6CM to 1KM

Flamborough Head

few steps to meet a path rising from the ravine. Follow it up left to join a track **D**.

A path opposite, signed to Flamborough, follows the field edge before becoming enclosed on its approach to Thornwick Farm. Turn left in front of the house, passing beside a white gate. At the corner of the walled garden go right and then swing left onto a drive in front of the shops serving the caravan site. Cross the main drive beside the security cabin and barrier to a short contained path and continue beyond at the edge of an open grass field. Meeting a lane at the far side **E**, follow it right. Where it subsequently bends past a junction, take the street ahead into Flamborough village.

Carry on forward into the square, turning left opposite the Royal Dog and Duck along Allison Lane. At the end **F**, go right and keep ahead at a crossroads, following the ongoing lane back to the car park above South Landing. ●

St Cuthbert's Cave

walk 6

Start

Holburn Grange
(signed St Cuthbert's
Cave from lane)

Distance

7 miles (11.3km)

Height gain

785 feet (240m)

Approximate time

4 hours

Route terrain

Generally clear tracks
and field paths

Parking

Car park at start

OS maps

Landranger 75
(Berwick-upon-Tweed),
Explorer 340 (Holy
Island and Bamburgh)

GPS waypoints

🖊 NU 051 351
Ⓐ NU 054 354
Ⓑ NU 059 352
Ⓒ NU 069 341
Ⓓ NU 083 350
Ⓔ NU 067 358
Ⓕ NU 060 352
Ⓖ NU 045 361

Set back from the Northumberland coast, a low range of sandstone heughs and craggy outcrops offer fabulous views to Holy Island and the Farne Islands, while to the south west are the distant Cheviots. One of the most dramatic viewpoints is Greensheen Hill, beneath which is a striking natural rock shelter, one of the traditional places where monks carrying St Cuthbert's relics paused during their wandering journey.

🖊 A hedged grass track rises beside the car park towards Greensheen Hill. Over a stile at the top Ⓐ, go right on a green track contouring the heath. Mounting another stile, walk within a fringe of pine woodland. After a few yards, bear off along a narrow path into the trees to the foot of St Cuthbert's Cave Ⓑ.

A place of pilgrimage

After St Cuthbert died in 687 on Inner Farne, his body was taken for interment at Lindisfarne. As tales of miracles spread, his tomb became a place of pilgrimage. But Viking raiders repeatedly harassed the monastery and, in 875, the monks fled in search of a safe haven, taking their most treasured possession, the miraculously still-preserved body of St Cuthbert. For seven troubled years, the brothers roamed northern England before settling at Chester-le-Street. In the 10th century, renewed raids again displaced the community and the monks took the saint to Ripon. Once the threat receded, they headed back towards Chester-le-Street, but the saint miraculously let it be known that he wished to be laid at Durham.

A broader track returns you to the main path. Continue left, exchanging the pine for larch, where a clearing reveals weatherworn outcrops of sandstone below more impressive cliffs. Keep going as the track bends into the thick of the forest, losing the views to the Cheviot Hills. At the crest of the hill, ignore a track leaving right and curve around to a gate leading from the trees Ⓒ.

As the path falls beside of open grazing, the expansive view is towards the sea and the Farne Islands. Beyond another patch of woodland, walk past a couple of sturdy barns to join an enclosed track that descends almost dead straight for the next ½ mile.

Reaching a junction beside a barn at Swinhoe Farm **D**, turn left towards Holburn. Approaching more timber, disregard tracks off right and swing past Swinhoe lakes. After gently climbing, the winding track leaves the trees. Stride on below a low gorse-covered heugh, eventually arriving at a gate and junction **E**.

Ignore the gate and instead, turn sharp left on a diagonal from the corner, a fingerpost pointing the way to St Cuthbert's Cave. Over a low rise, descend to a gate and strike across to a gated bridge at the foot of the next rough pasture. Maintain direction up the rising hillside, aiming for the right-hand forest edge on the skyline. At the crest, walk into the corner where fence and wall meet, there passing through a couple of gates **F**.

A narrow path follows the western side of the wall right to a ladder-stile, over which you can climb the outcrop for a grand view back to the coast. Return across the ladder-stile and continue along the heathery path, which snakes to the survey pillar topping Greensheen Hill.

St Cuthbert's Cave

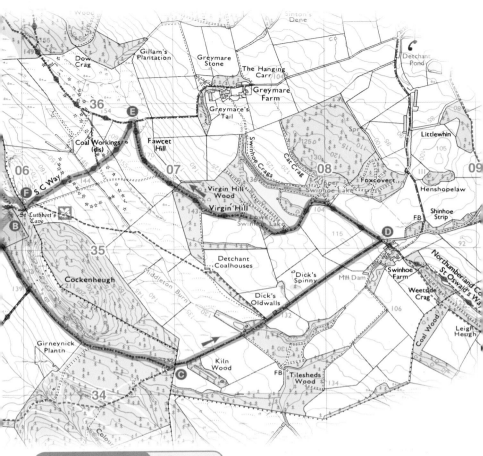

Having satiated yourself with the fine panorama, gently lose height along the ridge towards Holburn Moss. The broadening path swings left before Holburn Lake, closing with a wall and following it to a gate. Carry on downhill on the other side of the wall to join a track. Where that then swings towards the farm, leave through a field gate on the left **G**.

A trod shows the way at the edge of rough grazing, shortly winding with the fence to settle as a more prominent path along the bracken and gorse fringe below Greensheen Hill. After ½ mile, it brings you to the top of the track above Holburn Grange **A**, which leads back to the car park.

SCALE 1:25 000 or 2½ INCHES to 1 MILE 4CM to 1KM

walk 7

High and Low Force

Start
Bowlees Visitor Centre and café

Distance
8½ miles (13.7km)

Height gain
1,050 feet (320m)

Approximate time
4½ hours

Route terrain
Generally clear tracks and field paths

Parking
Car park at start

OS maps
Landranger 91 (Appleby-in-Westmorland) or 92 (Barnard Castle), Explorer OL31 (North Pennines - Teesdale & Weardale)

GPS waypoints
- NY 907 282
- Ⓐ NY 903 278
- Ⓑ NY 881 284
- Ⓒ NY 861 282
- Ⓓ NY 862 293
- Ⓔ NY 854 302
- Ⓕ NY 862 305
- Ⓖ NY 867 298
- Ⓗ NY 890 289

The walk upstream beside the Tees from Wynch Bridge is one of the best known in the North East, passing two of the region's most spectacular waterfalls, Low and High Force.

From Bowlees car park, cross the footbridge to the visitor centre, where an exhibition illustrates the area's history. Continue down the short lane to the main road and cross to a footpath opposite signed to Wynch Bridge. Walk down a couple of fields before descending through woodland to the bridge across the River Tees.

First wander upstream to look at the falls, which although not high are undoubtedly impressive, especially after heavy rain. Surging on a bed of hard whinstone, the river's peaty flow is fragmented and tumbles noisily over ragged steps to foam in

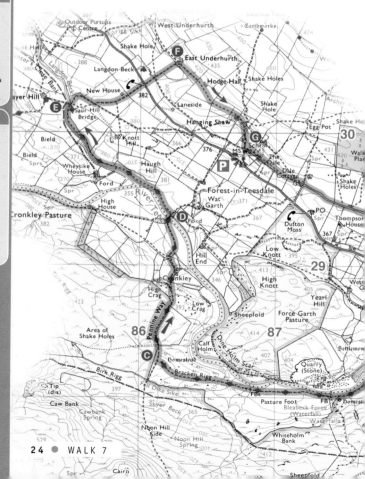

deep pools below. To the side runs a normally dry channel into which the river overspills during high flood.

Low Force

The bridge, then and now

The first bridge was slung across the gorge around 1741 by lead-miners, a precarious wooden footbed carried on chains and with only a single handrail for security. Despite collapsing in 1802 when nine harvesters attempted to cross, it continued in use until the Duke of Cleveland built the elegant suspension bridge that takes today's path to the far bank. However, regard the notice advising that only one person should venture over at a time.

Across the bridge **A**, turn upstream with the Pennine Way, shortly passing a pair of sculpted Swaledale sheep. In summer drifts of lilac scabious and yellow globeflowers border the path, and from the banks of the Tees you will see dippers and wagtails feeding

amongst crevices in the boulder-strewn bedrock. Through a succession of gates the path eventually leads to a second footbridge below Holwick Head House. However, remain on this bank, climbing above the river to enter the Moorhouse Upper Teesdale National Nature Reserve at the top of the rise. The ongoing path threads through the largest juniper wood in the country, some of the stunted trees being more than 250 years old. At a fork **B**, a viewpoint overlooking High Force lies a short distance to the right.

Back on the main path, continue upstream beside the bouldery bed of the river, shortly leaving the juniper wood behind. After almost ½ mile, opposite a working quarry on the north bank, the path crosses a bridge over Blea Beck. Leave the path and wander up beside the stream to see yet another splendid waterfall, Bleabeck Force.

Return to the Pennine Way and carry

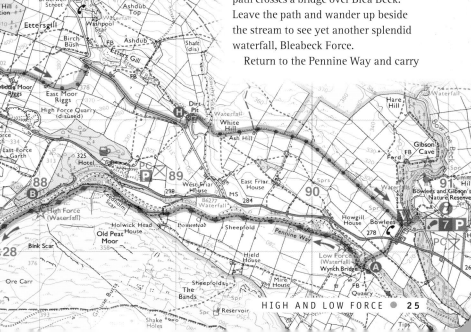

Looking down from High Force

High Force waterfall At 70 feet, the waterfall is not England's highest, but is certainly one of the most impressive, the Tees thundering over the black rock of the Whin Sill into the deep gorge below. *Take care for the cliff is unfenced and the rocks can be slippery.*

on up the valley, in a little while crossing two solid footbridges before curving away up steps and along a boardwalk onto Bracken Rigg. Pause as you climb for a grand view back down the Tees Valley.

The path crests at a point marked by two milestone-style waymarkers **C**. A path to the west slips off towards Cronkley Fell and Cauldron Snout, but your route is to the right, down the slabbed Pennine Way and up alongside a wall, presently going through a hand-gate and following the marshy path to a stile and gate below Cronkley Farm. Walk up to the right of the large barn and follow signs through the yard, leaving along the farm's access road into the valley. Cross the bridge **D** and immediately turn left along a path by the water. The views to Cronkley Scar across the confluence of the Tees with Langdon Beck can be stirring or sombre,

depending on the light.

Leave the Pennine Way at Saur Hill Bridge **E**, turning right along a farm lane signed to the Youth Hostel. Keep left at the junction, cross a cattle-grid and walk through to the road near to England's highest Youth Hostel at Langdon Beck. Follow the track opposite to East Underhurth Farm, passing through a gate below it. As the drive then turns sharp left, go through a gate to the right **F** and walk to Hodge Hall.

Fork right in front of the abandoned cottage to find a ladder-stile in the right-hand corner and head slightly left across a sloping field to a gate. A track leads to the houses and barns at Hanging Shaw. Join a metalled drive and pass through two gates to reach the tiny Forest-in-Teesdale Primary School on your left **G**.

Turn left along the lane behind the school and walk to its end. Continue forward on an overgrown path and then along the foot of fields, shortly walking behind Dale Cottage to meet the corner of a lane. Follow it ahead, later passing a melancholy old chapel before approaching the farm at Middle Moor Riggs. Bear left in front of the entrance to go through a gate. Carry on from field to field beside the right-hand wall. Beyond the deserted East Moor Riggs Farm, enter a final field. About halfway along swing left on a curving field track that drops to a gateway beside a cottage. Walk out to the lane and turn right.

After ½ mile at a junction **H**, fork left through the settlement of Dirt Pit, an unfortunate name for such a charming spot. It is actually a corruption of Deer Peth, a reference to an ancient hunting forest. Beyond a second stream, the way continues as a track, later falling gently through meadows back towards the wooded valley of Bow Lee Beck and the visitor centre. ●

Rock carvings on
Doddington Moor

Ancient Britain

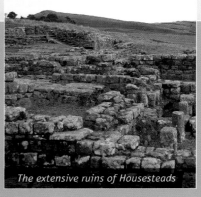

The extensive ruins of Housesteads

A warming climate at the end of the last ice age attracted modern man back to Britain. It had been assumed that these Stone Age peoples followed a purely nomadic hunter-gatherer lifestyle, but archaeological evidence suggests that plentiful local resources might have encouraged more permanent settlement and dwellings from 8500-8000 BC have been discovered at Starr Carr outside Scarborough and Howick near Craster.

But it was the emergence of agriculture around 4500 BC that truly tied man to a sedentary lifestyle and wrought change unsurpassed until the industrial age. Clearance for grazing and tillage led to the systematic removal of primeval forest that once blanketed all but the highest land. And with settlement came the first built structures to have survived as recognisable landscape features: standing stones, burial mounds, earthworks and field systems. Another 2,000 years or more would pass before bronze appeared, while the use of iron began only around 750 BC. Change was gradual, but different structural styles, together with the archaeological evidence painstakingly gleaned from excavation has pieced together our picture of life over this long period. However, without recourse to written records, which only appeared with the arrival of the Romans, our understanding is often limited and such sites may remain an enigma.

Northeastern England is rich in prehistoric sites. Amongst the most intriguing are numerous clusters of rock art scattered across the Northumberland hills. Cup and ring markings appear elsewhere in Britain as well as across Galicia, suggesting a cultural link, and were created during the Neolithic and Bronze ages. Many exist across **Doddington Moor**, in particular a large slab with groups of patterns, some of which, it has been suggested, might represent a map. Other nearby carvings worth seeking are at Lordenshaw and Roughting Linn.

At Doddington, the remains of a stone circle and enclosures are evidence of occupation during several ages, a characteristic of many sites. Although showing traces of earlier settlement, **Yeavering Bell** and the **Breamish Valley** are primarily known for the preponderance of Iron Age enclosures dotting the hills. Often on prominent summits, surrounded by earthworks, ditches and, sometimes, stone walls, they suggest defence and indeed many are referred to as 'forts'. Yet not all are strategically placed; platforms and hut circles within indicate living and storage areas, and many have associated field systems. Some sites may have served to coral livestock or for transhumance; temporary homes during seasonal migration to higher pastures. Subject to winter flooding, the valley bottoms were often marshy, but hillsides offered better prospects. Piles of stones can indicate fields cleared for cultivation and the terraces and ridges created by ploughing remain evident today. The practice continued into the medieval period and up and down the country, where not obliterated by modern ploughing, the gentle corrugations of 'rigg and furrow' hark back to the open field system that existed before enclosure.

Much older and perhaps dating from the Bronze Age, are the **Devil's Arrows** at Boroughbridge, massive menhirs whose alignment might have served as an astronomical calendar. Although now much weathered, the buried portions indicate the standing stones were carefully dressed to create a smooth surface. Their placement represented a significant investment in skill, time and planning and indicates an organised society.

The Romans first arrived under Julius Caesar in 55 BC, however, their conquest did not begin until AD 43, when troops under Plautius landed in the south east. They steadily extended their presence into Wales and towards Scotland, eventually achieving their northernmost victory against the Caledonians at the Battle of Mons in AD 84. The invaders consolidated their northern gains with two frontiers; between the Solway and Tyne and subsequently across the narrow waist of Scotland from the Clyde to the Forth. The Romans exploited the island's mineral resources, gold, iron, tin and lead and developed trade in wool, grain and other produce. Roman occupation brought not only a built infrastructure including a network of roads, but a new way of life and large sections of the indigenous population became 'Romanised'.

Aldborough was a thriving trading centre in the former territory of the Brigantes, the largest of the native tribes. It was close to Dere Street, which crossed the River Ure at present day Boroughbridge, where evidence of a military site has been discovered. The superb mosaic floors at Aldborough's museum hint of the luxury in which at least some of its inhabitants lived. Near Goathland is an impressive waterfall and one of the country's earliest railways, but high on the moor is arguably the best-preserved stretch of **Roman road** in Britain, which ran between Malton and Whitby, then important for its mineral, jet.

York was a strategically important town and so the presence of numerous Roman sites in the North East is not surprising. None is more famous, however, than **Hadrian's Wall**. The northernmost frontier of the Empire, it was a bold and formidable expression of Rome's dominance and remains one of the most evocative monuments of its age. The section adjoining **Housesteads** fort is dramatic and exploits the natural contours of the land to amplify its defensive capacity, while the fort gives a picture of what life was like in this far-flung corner of the Empire.

Ancient stones on Doddington Moor

Start
Doddington

Distance
4 miles (6.4km)

Height gain
540 feet (165m)

Approximate time
2½ hours

Route terrain
Hilly heathland and lane

Parking
Lay-by south of Doddington village cross or off main road in side lane

OS maps
Landranger 75 (Berwick-upon-Tweed), Explorer 340 (Holy Island & Bamburgh)

GPS waypoints
NT 999 323
Ⓐ NU 016 333
Ⓑ NU 013 323
Ⓒ NU 013 317
Ⓓ NU 012 313
Ⓔ NU 004 316

When Britain basked in a warmer climate than today, Doddington Moor was well populated with Bronze and Iron Age peoples who farmed the hillsides. They left their mark across what has now become heath in intriguing rock carvings, standing stones and settlement sites encircled by earthworks. The imposing cross set back from the road in the centre of the village, however, is recent. Designed by the local vicar in 1846, it stands above a natural spring, Dod Well.

Leave the main road beside the cross along a narrow lane signed to the Wooler Golf Club. Climbing gently away, it gives a view to the distant Lammermuir Hills. Where the lane eventually swings towards the golf club, keep ahead on an undulating sandy track.

Pass a large cattle shed and later dip beside a small plantation. Some 150 yds beyond the wood leave through a gate on the right Ⓐ. Strike sharp right across the cultivation in the direction indicated by the fingerpost to Weetwood Hill, on a bearing just west of south. Maintain the direction across the next rising pasture to a gate in the far corner.

Through that, follow the wall towards a clump of pine. As you approach the trees, look back right to a low bracken-covered hill. Ramparts and ditches surround the top, an Iron Age 'fort' that continued as a settlement site into the Roman period. Ignoring the clearer path that then bears off to the right Ⓑ, remain beside the wall. Over a stile pass onto bracken moor, accompanying the wall to a single standing stone Ⓒ. It is the sole survivor of a circle, the others lie fallen in the undergrowth.

Keep going over the crest, eventually reaching a corner with a fence Ⓓ. Turn right within and continue by the fence past a gate. Shortly, a cottage comes into view on the hillside in the middle distance. A waymark indicates a path leaving the fence, which rises across the slope of the hill. Mount a stile in an intervening boundary and continue below a low scar to the cottage, Shepherds House.

Some of the most intriguing rock art on the moor is to be found on the hill behind Shepherds House. Follow the track up beside the wall then bear off right on a narrow path to meet a broader grass track. Go left and immediately look for an

Enclosure

Cup marked
Rock

Doddington Dean
Wood

33

Ford
87

Cup & Ring
marked Rock Ⓐ

129 144 Spr

The Ringses
fort 154

Cup & Ring
marked Rocks

Cox
Grov
0145
(148)

00 78

Doddington
MP
PO

Cheviot
View

CH

Quarry

Wooler
Golf Club

01

144 140 135 125

Ⓑ

02

Bastle
(rems of)

8

Hall

Cup & Ring
marked Stone

Doddington Moor

09

Kitty's
Plantation Homestead

Horton Moor

32

Dod Law

Cup & Ring
marked Rock

Settlement

200

Enclosure

Hut Circles

Ⓒ

Stone Circle
(rems of)

Cup &
marked

Settlement

Shepherds
House Ⓔ

Enclosure

Ⓓ

155 157

Enclosure

31

Cup marked
Rocks

Cup & Ring
marked Rock

145

West
Plantation

143

Buttony

Cup & Ring
marked Rock

B 6525

Doddington

B 6352

00

99 98 97

09

96 95 94

93 92 91

90

Rock art The rock is carved with intriguing motifs and, like others roundabout, occupies a position of prominence. The intricate patterns have been fashioned by simply pounding the surface with a hard stone, sometimes taking advantage of the natural markings inherent in the rock.

0	200	400	600	800 METRES	1

KILOMETRES
MILES

0	200	400	600 YARDS	½

SCALE 1:25 000 or 2½ INCHES to 1 MILE 4CM to 1KM

exposed slab of bedrock to the right Ⓔ.

Return to the cottage and go right on a trod contouring the flank of the hill. Before long, the path begins to fall towards the village, the tall ruin of the bastle conspicuous amongst the buildings. Constructed in 1584 by Sir Thomas Grey of Chillingham and Wark as protection against raiding reivers, it was reputedly the last border stronghold to be built before the Union of the Crowns brought peace. It stood more or less complete until 1896, when a severe gale brought down the eastern end. Over a fence, follow a sparse line of hawthorn trees, holding your direction beyond its end. Breaking from the bracken, drop across pasture and then between clumps of gorse to find a stile at the bottom. Regaining the golf club lane, follow it left back to the village, where you can try real Northumbrian ice cream at North Doddington Farm, just off the main road along the lane towards Fenton.

Do these markings represent the plan of a village?

Yeavering Bell hill fort

Start

Ad Gefrin Monument, ¼ mile east of Old Yeavering

Distance

4 miles (6.4km)

Height gain

1,050 feet (320m)

Approximate time

2½ hours

Route terrain

Upland paths, steep climb and descent

Parking

Lay-by beside Ad Gefrin Monument

OS maps

Landranger 74 (Kelso & Coldstream), Explorer OL16 (The Cheviot Hills)

GPS waypoints

✍ NT 927 304
Ⓐ NT 916 292
Ⓑ NT 923 287
Ⓒ NT 928 294
Ⓓ NT 924 297

High on the northern edge of the Cheviot Hills overlooking the River Glen, Yeavering Bell is one of the most extensive Iron Age hilltop sites in the country. In the valley below Yeavering Bell, traces of even earlier settlement have been found, a Stone Age temple and a cemetery from the Bronze Age. Almost 2,500 years later, the plain was the site of an Anglo Saxon royal palace, where in 627, the early Christian missionary Paulinus came with King Edwin and his queen Aethelburgh, and conducted a mass baptism of Christian converts in the River Glen.

✍ Enter the field by the monument and go left beside the wall. A path from the corner leads back to the lane. Cross to a track opposite signed past the cottages of Old Yeavering to Torleehouse and, after winding around a barn, climb away along a shallow fold into the hills. Yeavering Bell rises steeply

> **Bird's eye discovery** Nothing remains above ground and the site of Ad Gefrin, which had been lost for centuries, was a chance discovery in 1949 from an aerial photograph. Subsequent excavation revealed traces of a small township centred upon a grand hall that could accommodate over 300 people. The settlement grew up around 580, and although twice destroyed by fire, was occupied until the middle of the 7th century.

to the left, while ahead are the even higher tops of Newton Tors.

After ¾ mile, immediately beyond a cattle-grid and gate Ⓐ, leave the track, swinging left up the edge of rough pasture, where scattered piles of stones were heaped up when the slope was first cleared for cultivation. Through a gate in the corner, follow a grass track back across the hillside, rising above a stand of conifers to a ladder-stile in the top wall. The ongoing path gains height to the right above a valley, continuing for ¼ mile to a low four-way signpost Ⓑ. The narrow path to the left, signed to Yeavering Bell and Gleadscleugh, soon arcs right through bracken to cross the stream flowing at the base of the valley. Climb to a waypost and then curve left to begin a steady ascent to the top of the hill.

The double summit is completely ringed by the fallen stones of a great defensive rampart defining the boundary of the

Burial mounds on neighbouring Kirknewton Hill

settlement. It once stood some 8 feet high enclosing some 5.6 hectares and is thought to have been built around 300 BC. Within were over 130 dwellings; timber and thatched huts footed on circular platforms, many of which can still be picked out. That so much wood was used in their construction suggests a very different landscape at the time, with extensive stands of woodland managed to provide both building timber and smaller poles for fencing, utensils and firewood. The inhabitants of the settlement were farmers, herding livestock and cultivating crop fields on the surrounding hillsides.

It was one of the largest Iron Age settlements in the north of Britain and its size undoubtedly reflected an importance in the social structure, the leader perhaps ruling the many smaller hilltop settlements in the area. An obvious inner bank and ditch surrounds the eastern summit, possibly denoting the house of the clan chief or even a sacred area, for the fell had been a revered site long before the fort builders came. The remains of an earlier burial cairn can be discerned on the eastern summit and a 'temple' below was aligned with the hilltop. But while further archaeological exploration may yield more tantalising clues as to the site's history, the full story may forever remain an enigmatic puzzle.

After exploring the site, leave through a break in the mid-point of the northern wall, where there is a waypost

C. A narrow path drops steeply to the left across the flank of the hill, eventually meeting the corner of a wall **D**. Cross a stile over a fence beside it and continue downhill next to the wall. Farther down, mount a ladder-stile beside a gate on the right and walk away on a rough track that quickly disintegrates to a trod. Wayposts guide your descent across the lower slopes of the fell, a grass track finally leading to a ladder-stile beside the barn at Old Yeavering. Reverse your outward steps past the cottages and back to the lay-by.

On top of Yeavering Bell

Iron Age settlements in the Breamish Valley

walk 10

Start
Ingram Bridge

Distance
6 miles (9.7km)

Height gain
1,300 feet (395m)

Approximate time
3½ hours

Route terrain
Upland paths, steep climbs

Parking
Car park by Ingram Bridge

OS maps
Landranger 81 (Alnwick & Morpeth), Explorer OL16 (The Cheviot Hills)

GPS waypoints
　　NU 017 163
Ⓐ NU 007 163
Ⓑ NT 998 163
Ⓒ NU 000 155
Ⓓ NU 004 146
Ⓔ NU 007 140
Ⓕ NU 013 144
Ⓖ NU 009 155

Today, only a handful of cottages and farms huddle within the fold of the Breamish Valley as it breaks from the Cheviot Hills, but 2,500 years ago, the area supported a larger population, whose settlements ranged high onto the surrounding slopes. Even earlier are burial cairns and traces of Bronze Age civilisation. This fine walk winds by half a dozen Iron Age enclosures in as many miles, tangible relics of vibrant and thriving communities.

Before starting out, visit the nearby National Park Visitor Centre, where there is an interesting display describing the rich history of the area and will help give context to the ancient sites visited during the walk. Then, follow the lane towards Hartside and Linhope for ½ mile to a car park beside Bulby's Wood. Take the footpath opposite the entrance Ⓐ, signed to Brough Law, which climbs through the bracken. Intercepting a broader path, follow it right, rising steadily along a grassy ridge. There is a grand view along the valley and closer to are the scattered stones of a Bronze Age settlement. At a fork beyond the upper corner of a forest plantation, bear right, making for the top of Brough Law Ⓑ.

> **Brough Law** The stone rampart surrounding the top remains an impressive sight and in places a second wall and ditch can be seen. Inside several hut platforms are evident, the remnants of circular low-walled buildings that were roofed with wood and thatch.

Retreat through the entrance and head half-right, dropping through an outer earthwork to join the main path at a waymark. The trail meanders south across the grassy hillside towards Ewe Hill. Reaching a wayposted junction after ¼ mile, bear right Ⓒ, but then at the next junction, go left, resuming the climb around the flank of the hill. Eventually meeting the corner of a fence, keep ahead, walking to the next corner, which overlooks the deep valley head of Middle Dean. Cross left over a stile and head downhill above the gully, shortly reaching a double-banked enclosure hard up against the lip of the valley and which extends to the left.

At a waypost **D**, double back right along the steep valley side. Crossing a stile, arc around to a second stile and climb away, occasional waymarks guiding you onto the next hill, Cochrane Pike. A vague earthwork surrounds the summit plateau, in the centre of which stands a waymark **E**. The ongoing route is to the left, but first walk ahead to witness the tremendous view and find, as the ground falls away, a more clearly defined earthwork and the remains of four small huts.

Retrace your steps to the waypost **E** and turn right, following the path gently down the eastern flank of Cochrane Pike. Ignoring crossing paths,

descend to a shallow saddle, where a low embankment perhaps marks the boundary between two settlements. Keep ahead, gaining height to the next camp on top of Wether Hill **F**. Although not particularly large it has an impressive double embankment and again hut circles are to be seen.

From the top, turn left (north west) through a gap in the defence towards a marker post. Carry on ahead with the steepening slope, the path later running beside the deepening gully of Corbie Cleugh into the bottom of the main valley. Prominent on the opposite hillside are parallel strips of cultivation terraces where crops of oats and barley were grown. Over to the left is another view of the settlement above Middle Dean passed earlier.

Through a gate in the bottom fence, climb away to the top of a rise and continue across the undulations of cultivation ridges. The earliest terraces have been dated to the Bronze Age, but others are Iron Age and even medieval. After crossing a stile, the path once

Looking back to Brough Law

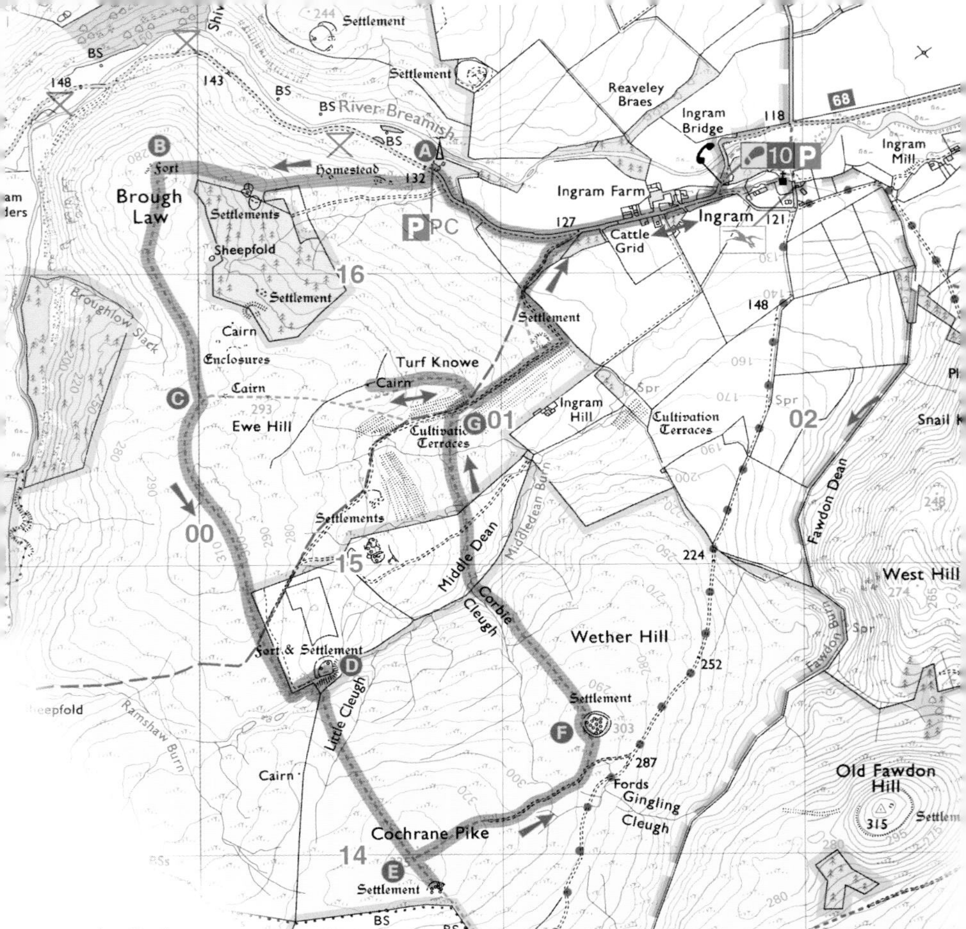

again climbs
to meet a broad
bridlepath **G**. Cross
to the narrow path
opposite and carry on up
through bracken, shortly swinging
left as it joins a broader swathe. Head
up the fellside between two hillocks to
another small enclosure higher up.

Retrace your steps downhill, visiting
the hillocks on either side as you
descend. On the left is a circular cairn,
in which were found two cist burials,
while that on the right has an unusual
tri-radial form. These have been dated
to around 2000 BC, but the site also
revealed flints from the Mesolithic era,
suggesting a camp used by early
hunter-gatherers.

Walk back to the waypost **G** beside
the bridlepath and go left. The track
swings past the final Iron Age site of the
walk, Ingram Hill. It is the lowest of the
hillforts to be found in the Breamish
Valley, although the remains of the
rectangular buildings identifiable
within are from a much later date. The
track eventually emerges onto the lane,
which, to the right, leads back to the
car park.

SCALE 1:25000 or 2½ INCHES to 1 MILE 4CM to 1KM

Start

Boroughbridge

Distance

4 miles (6.4km)

Height gain

150 feet (45m)

Approximate time

2 hours

Route terrain

Riverside paths and lanes

P Parking

Boroughbridge

OS maps

Landranger 99 (Northallerton & Ripon), Explorer 299 (Ripon & Boroughbridge)

GPS waypoints

SE 396 666
A SE 391 664
B SE 399 666
C SE 398 670
D SE 411 667
E SE 405 661

The Devil's Arrows and Aldborough

After a short detour to an impressive group of standing stones dating from around 2000 BC, this undemanding walk takes a roundabout route beside the River Ure to nearby Aldborough, whose Roman past is revealed in a small museum.

The pleasant town of Boroughbridge grew around a Norman river crossing, just upstream of the Roman town. The bridge itself has been rebuilt many times during the centuries, the most notable instance following collapse in 1945, when a transporter carrying an 85-ton load optimistically attempted to cross.

The walk begins from the ornate fountain in St James' Square. To see the Devil's Arrows, cross to The Black Bull and walk along St Helena, branching left to the main road. Go left and then almost immediately right along Roecliffe Lane. You will find the 'arrows' a little less than ¼ mile along **A**, two in the right-hand field and the other to the left of the lane.

Pillars lost in time

It is thought there were originally five pillars, one lost in time and another broken during the 16th century to provide stone for a bridge across the River Tutt. A plausible theory suggests an alignment with midsummer moonrise, but their true purpose will never be known. They are none the less impressive; the largest standing over 22 feet high and taller than any other in the country apart from Stonehenge.

Return to St James' Square and continue past The Malt Shovel along Aldborough Road. Where it shortly bends, take the minor road towards Aldborough, walking for another

Tessellated floor - Aldborough

150 yds to a footpath signed through a kissing-gate on the left **B**. It leads across the fields to the River Ure.

Climbing onto the embankment **C**, follow the meandering riverside path downstream for a little over 1¼ miles until you eventually drop out onto a track **D**.

Follow it right to meet a lane and go right again towards Aldborough. Approaching the village, branch off left and then keep left to pass the central open green. Continue up to the top of the street, following it around right to a junction. The entrance to the Roman town and museum is then just to the left **E**.

The Devil's Arrows

Isurium Brigantium The Romans established Isurium Brigantium in AD 71, guarding the point at which Dere Street from York crossed the river. A civil settlement developed around the military encampment and after the Romans left Britain, it continued as the principal town of the Romanised Brigantes. Fragments of the walls remain, but the finest treasures are two splendid mosaic pavements.

Leaving the museum, follow the street down into the village past the other side of the green where stands a tall maypole. Keep left past the church to meet the main lane. The pub lies just to the right, otherwise turn left to return to Boroughbridge.

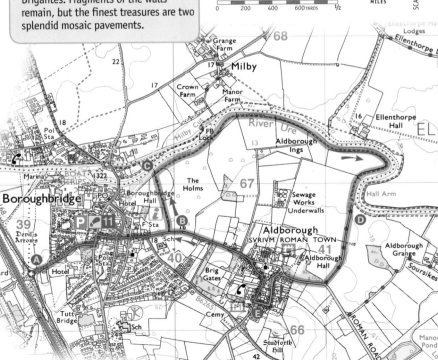

walk 12

The Roman road on Wheeldale Moor

Start
Goathland

Distance
7½ miles (12.1km)

Height gain
1,380 feet (420m)

Approximate time
4½ hours

Route terrain
Some rugged paths and steep climbs

Parking
National Park car park

OS maps
Landranger 94 (Whitby & Esk Dale), Explorer OL27 (North York Moors - Eastern area)

GPS waypoints
NZ 833 013
Ⓐ NZ 821 020
Ⓑ NZ 824 011
Ⓒ NZ 814 003
Ⓓ SE 808 999
Ⓔ SE 811 990
Ⓕ SE 807 980
Ⓖ SE 815 987
Ⓗ NZ 827 007

Warning
Do not attempt after heavy rain!

Dramatic scenery and considerable historic appeal are features of this superb walk, which winds through a narrow, wooded gorge past a spectacular waterfall before climbing onto the open moor where there is an impressive stretch of Roman road. Also passed along the way is a long incline which connected the two halves of the railway through the valley, one 250 feet above the other.

Note: the route beside West Beck past Mallyan Spout can be slippery and dangerous, care is required and you should stick to the recognised path. Indeed, after heavy rain, the gorge may be impassable, as will the stepping stones across Wheeldale Beck below the Roman road. If this is the case, the onward walk should not be attempted and return to Goathland by following the signed path left at Ⓑ.

In Goathland, the moors are inseparable from the village. Sheep graze its spacious commons and the widely spaced cottages are strung out along a ¾-mile ridge above the valleys of Eller Beck to the east and West Beck to the west. The squat, solid-looking parish church at the southern end of the village, which was built in 1896, harmonises perfectly with its attractive surroundings.

The walk starts at the car park, from which you should turn left along Beck Hole Road. After 100 yds, go left again through a kissing-gate, signed 'Grosmont Rail Trail', and follow a grassy path down to a road. Cross and continue along a steadily downhill gravel track opposite. Part of the original Whitby - Pickering Railway built by George Stephenson and

The historic North York Moors Railway

The Roman road across Wheeldale Moor

opened in 1836, this mile-long section to Beck Hole descends a 1-in-15 incline.

> **A long haul** The climb between Beck Hole and Goathland was a major obstacle for the railway engineers because the slope was too steep, both for the early horse-drawn carriages and the later steam-powered locomotives. Hauling the carriages up and down the incline by means of a cable system solved the problem. However, this proved both unsatisfactory and unsafe, and so in 1865, blasting a cutting through the rocks to the north created an alternative route, the one still used by the present North York Moors Railway.

At the bottom, pass through a gate to Incline Cottage Ⓐ. Go left opposite Incline Cottage, signed 'The Mallyan', and continue through a kissing-gate at the edge of a meadow above West Beck. For the next ¾ mile, the sometimes steeply climbing and falling path passes through successive gates as it makes its way up the narrow, wooded valley, eventually leading to a junction by a bench, where a path is signed off left to Goathland Ⓑ.

The next mile lies along the gorge above West Beck, where *slippery rocks can sometimes make the way dangerous, therefore be careful as you proceed.* However, it is an exceptionally beautiful place, the highlight being the impressive 70ft-fall of Mallyan Spout, just a little higher up the ravine. Climbing beyond, the path briefly crosses to the opposite bank, before returning to continue upstream, finally emerging over a stile onto a lane by a bridge Ⓒ.

Follow it up left to a bend, there turning through a gate on the right from which a waymarked track drops towards a ford. However, just before the river, bear left over a footbridge and then go left again past the front of a house to reach a field gate just beyond. Walk along the length of a narrow field, leaving through a gate on the right near its far end to continue up through a wood on a stony path. Through another gate above, keep going in the same direction by trees and then a wall to the top corner of the field. Turn left through a gate there and continue along the right-hand perimeter of the next field, passing through a gate on the right when you reach its far corner. Now

Mallyan Spout

something of the history of the 'Roman' road, which then lies ahead.

Follow the roadway across the open and breezy expanse of Wheeldale Moor, shortly climbing a stile. Keep going for another 300 yds, and then turn sharp left **F** along a discernible path. Initially through the heather, the way soon becomes rocky as it descends below Skivick Crag to stepping stones across Wheeldale Beck. On the opposite bank, continue over a stile, but at the corner of a wall, go left on a path to Wheeldale Lodge. Carry on along a track over a rise, dropping to cross a beck by Hunt House **G**.

For the inexperienced, navigating the next section in mist might be difficult, in which case, simply keep with the lane back to Goathland. Otherwise, leave the track immediately beyond the bridge, bearing right onto the moor and rising beside a ditch to join a grassy track higher up. Vague tracks and sheep paths confuse the way ahead, but keep your upward direction, bearing right again and making for a prominent cairn on the rocky skyline ahead. Beyond the cairn, a clear path runs to the left along the top of the ridge, giving magnificent views across the valley on a clear day. Keep going for a little over ¼ mile passing several small cairns before reaching a larger one, set back to the left of the obvious path. Bear off left past it, and follow an indistinct path that drops across the slope, to join a more prominent track below, which

climb ahead at the field edge, exiting at the top onto a tarmac track **D**, from where there is a glorious panorama across the valley.

Walk left along the track for just over ¼ mile through gates to Hazel Head Farm. Keep going past the buildings, leaving through another at the far end. The way continues as a descending path between hedge banks, dropping through gates and passing into trees at the bottom above a brook **E**. Head upstream to cross a footbridge and continue a little farther on the opposite bank to a stile. Go left to join a track climbing over rough grassland above a wall. Mounting another stile, follow a wall around left to pass through a gate at the top, where a plaque describes

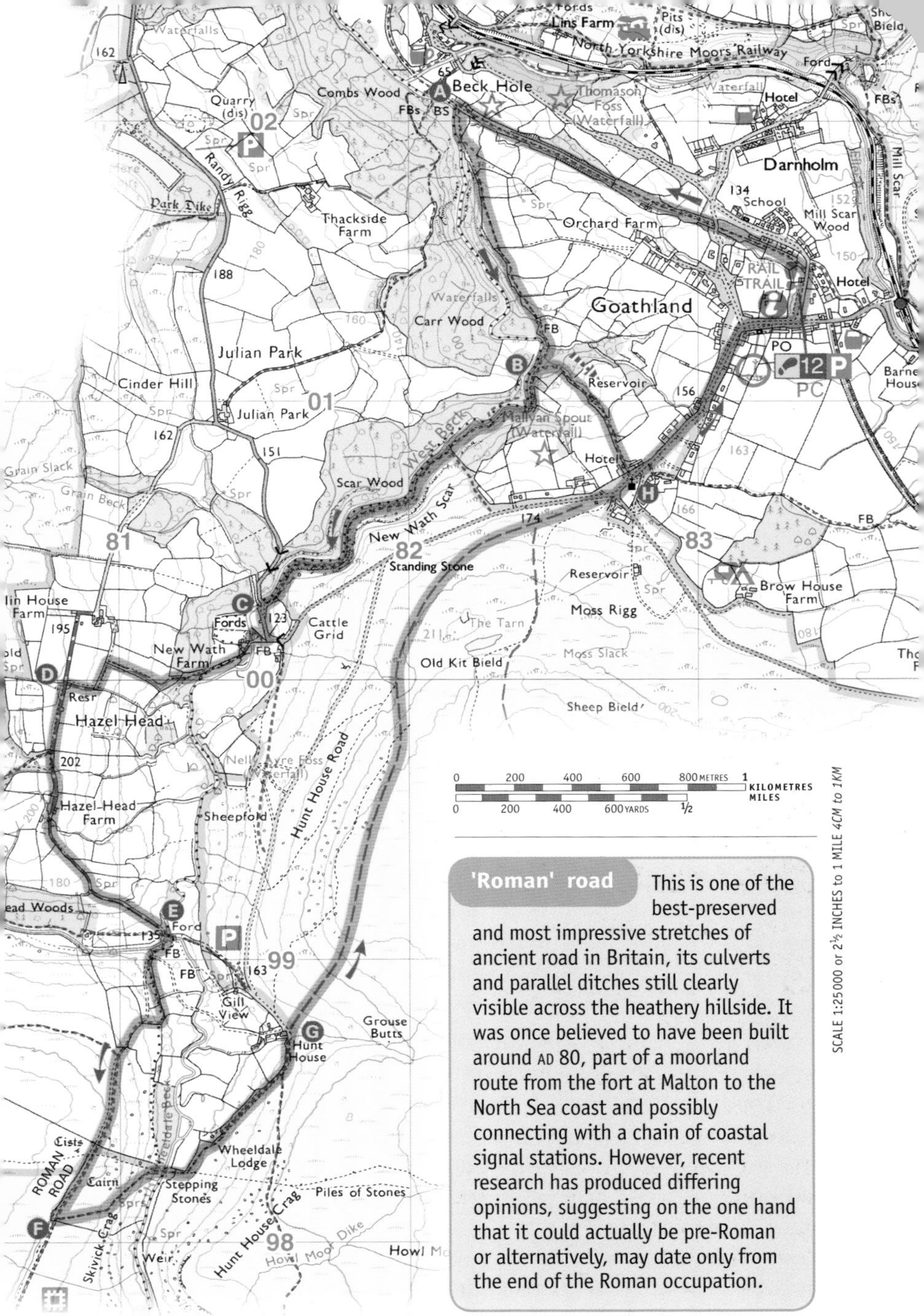

Map labels (selected):

162 · Waterfalls · Fords · Lins Farm · Pits (dis) · North Yorkshire Moors Railway · Ford · Sh... Bield

Quarry (dis) · Combs Wood · FBs · BS · A · Beck Hole · Thomason Foss (Waterfall) · Hotel · FBs

02 · P · Randy Rigg · Darnholm · 134 School · Mill Scar Wood · Mill Scar · Hotel

Park Dike · Thackside Farm · Orchard Farm · RAIL TRAIL · 150

188 · Carr Wood · Waterfalls · Goathland · FB · RAIL TRAIL · Hotel

Julian Park · 01 · Julian Park · Reservoir · 156 · i · PO · 12 · P · PC · Barne House

Cinder Hill · 162 · 151 · Spr · Mallyan Spout (Waterfall) · Hotel · 163

Grain Slack · Grain Beck · Scar Wood · New Wath Scar · 174 · H · 166 · FB

81 · 82 · Standing Stone · Reservoir · 83 · X · Brow House Farm

lin House Farm · 195 · Fords · 123 · Cattle Grid · Moss Rigg · 081

D · Resr · New Wath Farm · FB · 00 · The Tarn · 211 · Old Kit Bield · Moss Slack · The

Hazel Head · 202 · Sheepfold · Nell... Eyre Foss (Waterfall) · Sheep Bield

Hazel Head Farm · 180 · Hunt House Road

ead Woods · E · Ford · 135 · FB · P · FB · 99 · 163 · Gill View · G · Hunt House · Grouse Butts

Cists · ROAD · Cairn · Stepping Stones · Wheeldale Lodge · Piles of Stones

ROMAN · F · 98 · Skivick Crag · Weir · Hunt House Crag · Hovel Moor Dike · Howl M...

Scale:
0 200 400 600 800 metres 1 KILOMETRES
0 200 400 600 YARDS ½ MILES
SCALE 1:25000 or 2½ INCHES to 1 MILE 4CM to 1KM

'Roman' road This is one of the best-preserved and most impressive stretches of ancient road in Britain, its culverts and parallel ditches still clearly visible across the heathery hillside. It was once believed to have been built around AD 80, part of a moorland route from the fort at Malton to the North Sea coast and possibly connecting with a chain of coastal signal stations. However, recent research has produced differing opinions, suggesting on the one hand that it could actually be pre-Roman or alternatively, may date only from the end of the Roman occupation.

leads ahead past the head of a shallow valley. The way, again clear, then curves gently to the right, gradually closing with the lane below. Soon the moorland is left behind and a grassy path takes you down to the road. Go right to a junction and bear left past Goathland's church and the Mallyan Spout Hotel **H** for the final ¾ mile walk back through the village to the car park.

walk 13

Hadrian's Wall and Housesteads

Start

Steel Rigg, ¾ mile north of Once Brewed National Park Information Centre

Distance

6 miles (9.7km)

Height gain

950 feet (290m)

Approximate time

3½ hours

Route terrain

Moorland and rugged paths

Parking

Car park at start

OS maps

Landranger 86 (Haltwhistle & Brampton) or 87 (Hexham & Haltwhistle), Explorer OL43 (Hadrian's Wall – Haltwhistle & Hexham)

GPS waypoints

NY 751 676
Ⓐ NY 780 686
Ⓑ NY 788 687
Ⓒ NY 778 690
Ⓓ NY 771 684

Hadrian visited Britannia in 122 to inspect the northernmost province of his empire following a revolt amongst the Brigantes. Intending to secure rather than expand, he commissioned the wall between the Tyne and Solway. Largely complete by 128, it consolidated the existing frontier defined by the Stanegate, a Roman road connecting the forts at Corbridge and Carlisle. Milecastles, interspersed along its 80-mile length), guarded gateways, some of which were extended into full-sized forts; Chesters, Housesteads and Birdoswald now being the best known.

From a gate at the rear of the car park, a path leads to the Roman wall. Go left into Peel Gap and climb steeply to a ladder-stile. Running along the lofty cliffs the wall, restored to an impressive shoulder height, commanded the rolling countryside to the north, which, despite their best efforts, the Romans never fully wrested from the Caledonians.

In the next gap, Cat Stairs, wild flowers flourish in the poor soil, improved by lime that has leached from the crumbling mortar and infill. After another sharp climb, the way drops to Castle Nick, which is protected by a milecastle.

Later dipping again, the path cuts through to the outer flank of the wall. Clamber up to continue above

The wall As well as being a strategic defence and awesome symbol of the Roman Empire's might, the wall served to regulate trade and the comings and goings across the frontier. The forts served as customs posts where goods could be taxed and civilian settlements grew up around them to take advantage of passing trade.

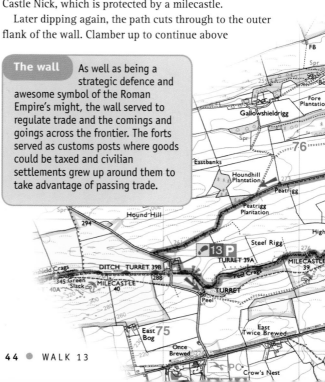

Milecastle 39

Construction The eastern portion was constructed in stone, and the Pennine section along the scarps of the Great Whin Sill must have appeared invincible. Beyond Birdoswald, a scarcity of outcropping limestone, needed for mortar, may have been a reason for the western section being built in turf. The vallum followed later, a wide ditch flanked by two embankments and possibly defined a military zone behind the wall.

Crag Lough before descending gently through pine woodland towards the far end of the lough. Leaving the trees, walk on to intersect a track from Hotbank Farm, there slipping back behind the wall to skirt the farm and the

SCALE 1:27777 or 2¼ INCHES to 1 MILE 3.6CM to 1KM

| 0 | 200 | 400 | 600 | 800 METRES | 1 |
| KILOMETRES |
| MILES |
| 0 | 200 | 400 | 600 YARDS | ½ |

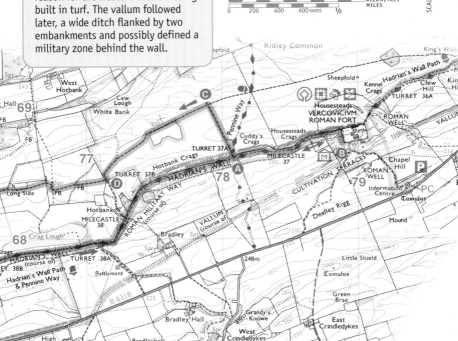

grassed ruin of another milecastle.

A strenuous climb preludes the airy stretch above Hotbank Crags before the wall drops to Ranishaw Gap . The return route lies over the stile to the left, but first, continue beside the wall over Cuddy's Crags and past the milecastle on Housesteads Crags to Housesteads Fort .

The Roman fort, Vercovicium, overlooks a gateway beside Knag Burn and slightly post-dates the wall. One of the best-preserved sites along its length, the barracks housed some 800 infantry, overseen by a commandant whose residence stood at the centre of the complex. Perhaps its most famous feature is the latrine block, but there were also store houses, a hospital and administration buildings. A civilian settlement developed outside the walls, where a bathhouse has been identified.

Return to cross the stile at Ranishaw Gap and, ignoring the Pennine Way sign, head straight out from the wall, following the course of a dilapidated field boundary to a substantial limekiln ¼ mile away . There, turn left, following a vague track along the top of a low escarpment. Passing a plantation, bear slightly left, shortly picking up a more distinct track that curves left to a gate at the end of a wall behind Hotbank Farm .

Instead of passing through, cross a ladder-stile to the right and strike out across a large pasture. Keep going to the far side of a second field, where a fingerpost directs you right to another stile. Resume your westerly heading past Crag Lough, side-stepping an enclosure and a couple of farm sheds. Carry on beside the ongoing wall, the way later materialising as a track that rises beside Peatrigg Plantation. It then winds down into the base of the valley, eventually meeting a lane. Climb left back to the car park at Steel Rigg.

Hypocausts at Housesteads

14 Fountains Abbey
Parkland and field paths
5¾ miles (9.3km)
3 hours

15 The lost village of Wharram Percy
Lanes and hilly field paths
2¾ miles (4.4km)
1½ hours

16 Dunstanburgh Castle
Well used paths
4¾ miles (7.6km)
2½ hours

17 Rievaulx and Helmsley
Clear tracks, paths and lane
3¾ miles (6km)
2 hours

18 Lindisfarne – a castle and a priory
Coastal paths, rocky beaches and sand dunes
5½ miles (8.9km)
3 hours

19 Castle Howard
Field paths and estate tracks
5½ miles (8.9km)
3 hours

20 The ancient city of Durham
Field and riverside paths
5½ miles (8.9km)
3 hours

Soaring columns in Fountains Abbey

Churches, Castles & Houses

Churches, Castles & Houses

Inside Crook Hall

After the Romans departed around 410, the legacy of their civilisation fell into decline. Angle and Saxon settlers, first brought as mercenaries by the Romans began to assert their dominance. The great Anglo-Saxon kingdoms emerged, with Northumbria stretching north from the Humber. Christianity had arrived with the Romans, but England remained largely Pagan until the arrival of Pope Gregory's missionaries in 596. Paulinus baptised the Northumbrian king, Edwin, at York in 627, but the spread of the new religion throughout the kingdom was down to Edwin's successor, Oswald. Converted during exile in Scotland into the 'Celtic' tradition, Oswald founded a proselytising monastery on Lindisfarne.

In 793, Scandinavian warriors attacked the island; the Viking Age had begun. Over time, attacks intensified and the raiders began staking claim on the land. By 865, they had taken York – Jorvik, and soon all of Northumbria was brought within the Danelaw. The monks were eventually forced to abandon their island monastery, taking with them their most precious treasure, the body of St Cuthbert. The relics were finally laid to rest at Durham in 995, but it was not until 1093 that the monks returned to their beloved island.

By then the country had fallen to another invading force, the Normans, themselves ironically of Viking stock. But despite his decisive victory at Hastings, William faced stiff resistance in the north, with rebellions gaining support from the Danes. His retribution was vicious and during the winter of 1069-70, he utterly devastated the land and its people between the Humber and the Tees. Replacing local overlords with his own men, he established the Prince Bishops at Durham to exert control over the northern borderlands. However, four centuries would pass before the union of the Scottish and English crowns finally brought peace and the north is littered with castles, bastles and pele towers, the stark architecture of defence.

Everywhere, the Norman warlords consolidated their positions with motte-and-bailey castles of earth and wood, those of strategic value being rebuilt in stone. Durham, Pickering, York, Alnwick and **Helmsley** were some of the first, with others like Scarborough and **Dunstanburgh** following as the medieval period unfolded. The picturesque fort on Lindisfarne, however, is much later, founded in 1570 to offer protection from sea-born raiders. The continuing threat of Scottish and foreign attack, rebellion and civil war provided an ongoing raison d'être for these strongholds and it was not until the end of the Cromwellian wars, that powerful cannon finally rendered them obsolete.

The medieval period saw the

blossoming of a different type of architecture too, for the Normans and their successors were also great ecclesiastical builders. The next centuries saw a wave of monastic foundation and flurry of church building. The ancient monasteries at Whitby and **Lindisfarne** and the great minster at York were among the first to be rebuilt. Others soon followed like the grand new cathedral at **Durham**. The contemplative and (at least initially) austere lifestyle of monasticism dictated that abbeys should be free from distraction and many such as Rievaulx and Fountains were deliberately located in remote regions. In fact, Byland, a neighbour of **Rievaulx**, had to be re-sited so that the monks were not disturbed by each other's bells. To support their building and maintenance, endowments of money and land accompanied the foundation. The religious communities became skilled managers of their assets, overseeing vast sheep runs, productive farms and mineral resources.

But what of ordinary people? Although many of today's towns and villages have evolved from a medieval past, later construction and redevelopment have largely obliterated what went before. Deserted villages and settlements can be found in fields across the country, but it is often difficult to envisage their form. At **Wharram Percy**, the humps and hollows of buildings and streets are quite distinct and detailed archaeological excavation has provided a valuable insight into peasant life during the Middle Ages. The cause of abandonment is often a mystery, depopulation during the Black Death in 1349 being commonly cited. But this is not always the case and other explanations given are the overuse of marginal land or a whimsical lord of the manor improving the view from his mansion. Wharram Percy, however, seems to have been a victim of 15th-century economics, when sheep and wool production became more profitable to the landowner than arable farming.

The region is well populated with medieval architecture, but with the relative stability of the Tudor period, the landed gentry increasingly sought comfort and befitting grandeur in their homes. Over the next two hundred years, the rich created ever-more sumptuous mansions, emphasising their position in society. The Percy's have held Alnwick since the beginning of the 14th century, and over the centuries have transformed its austere fortress fabric into an opulent palace. Others were built from scratch, one of the grandest being **Castle Howard**, which took a century from conception to completion in 1811. In many ways it represents the culmination of the English country house and a tour of its lavishly decorated and furnished rooms is not to be missed. The hall at **Fountains** was from a different age. Begun in 1598, it was finished in only six years; a beautiful example of the Jacobean style. It stands within the estate of **Fountains Abbey**, a Cistercian house founded in 1132. The manor's architect, Robert Smythson, who had trained as a stonemason at Longleat, designed several other magnificent mansions including Burton Agnes Hall in the Yorkshire Wolds, and here reused much stone from the abbey ruins.

walk 14

Fountains Abbey

Start

Fountains Abbey

Distance

5¾ miles (9.3km)

Height gain

550 feet (165m)

Approximate time

3 hours

Route terrain

Parkland and field paths

Parking

Visitor Centre main car park

OS maps

Landranger 99 (Northallerton & Ripon), Explorer 298 (Nidderdale)

GPS waypoints

SE 271 687
Ⓐ SE 274 692
Ⓑ SE 290 702
Ⓒ SE 291 689
Ⓓ SE 282 692
Ⓔ SE 286 685
Ⓕ SE 272 679

Fountains Abbey shelters in a valley below the eastern fringe of the Pennines. Medieval monks first tamed the landscape, but the parkland and water gardens of Studley Royal are a later aesthetic rather than practical creation undertaken by John Aislabie and his son William during the 18th century. This walk crosses the deer park to return through the picturesque lower valley and over the higher ground to the south.

Emerging from the car park opposite a roundabout, turn right along a hedged bridleway that parallels the road. Just after the entrance to the 'Pheasantries', the path ends at a gate into Studley Park by the Obelisk Ⓐ. Follow the drive through the estate, passing St Mary's Church and the Chorister's House. A splendid avenue falls away, lined mainly with lime but distinctive too is sweet chestnut. It swings to cut a dead straight line across the park, where herds of fallow deer and a few sika graze both the grass and the leaves on the trees, neatly pruning their lower branches to a uniform height above the ground.

Towards the far end of the avenue, about 500 yds before it reaches a park gate, bear off left along a mown path, which rises between massive chestnut trees to a small gate in the boundary wall. Carry on between fields and then at the back of walled cottage gardens to emerge onto a lane in the pleasing estate hamlet of Studley Roger Ⓑ.

Turning right, walk through the settlement and past the main entrance to the park. Beyond, the lane deteriorates to a track, which gently climbs and eventually leads past Plumpton Hall. The view left is to Ripon in the middle distance, where the cathedral's squat towers rise as an obvious landmark. Over the crest, the way enters a wood, dropping to meet the River Skell at a ford Ⓒ.

Remaining on this bank, swing with the track to follow the river upstream and, passing through a gate, continue along a meadow at the base of a narrow, twisting valley. The river repeatedly meanders from side to side, the path hopping across a succession of quaint stone bridges and eventually leading to a wooden span above a dam footing Studley's ornamental lakes Ⓓ.

To continue, turn back from the bridge, but instead of retracing your steps along the valley, bear right onto a track curving around at the edge of an enclosed wood. Through a high gate at the top, stride across open parkland. Approaching a deer fence, bend right beside it and carry on beyond its end to

The Abbey Although today roofless, the great abbey at Fountains remains a splendid sight. It was founded in 1132, with 13 dissident monks from the Benedictine abbey of St Mary's in York seeking a return to the simpler life originally envisaged by St Benedict.

a dilapidated stone gateway flanked by two small roofless lodges at the far side of the park **E**.

Leaving the open grassland, turn right onto a woodland path, emerging once more into pasture at the far end. Walk ahead, rising to meet a track, which follows a hedge on towards Hill House Farm. In the yard, markers direct you left and then right past the barns. As you approach the farmhouse, bear left down to a gate and into a field. Go right past farm buildings to join a field track and carry on through a gate. A little farther on, immediately after passing a gate the track turns left towards the corner of a wood. Re-entering parkland, keep ahead initially by the wood. As that curves away,

drift over to follow the remains of the old abbey boundary wall on the left, the higher ground allowing a view across to the ruins of the abbey and Fountains Hall, nestling in the valley below.

The way eventually emerges onto Fountains Lane **F**, where you should turn right. At a junction, keep right and cross a bridge over the River Skell in front of Abbey Cottages, continuing up the hill beyond. At the top, fork off right along a bridleway, soon joining a metalled drive, which leads ahead back to the car park entrance. However, a hedged path accompanies it on the left, so you can avoid most of the tarmac. ●

SCALE 1:25000 or 2½ INCHES to 1 MILE 4CM to 1KM

```
0      200    400    600    800 METRES    1
                                          KILOMETRES
                                          MILES
0      200    400    600 YARDS    ½
```

The lost village of Wharram Percy

Excavation and research spanning more than 50 years has made Wharram Percy the most famous of Britain's 3,000 or so deserted medieval villages. It is the focal point of this short but spectacular walk in the Yorkshire Wolds, which encircles the dale to approach from the south from where the best view of the site is to be had.

Turn right from the car park along the lane and follow it for ½ mile to a sharp right-hand bend. Where the lane subsequently curves left, keep ahead through a gate Ⓐ along a track signed as the Centenary Way. Beyond a wood, walk on along the top of an expansive field to exit through a gate at its far end Ⓑ.

Joining the Yorkshire Wolds Way, swing right towards Wharram Percy on a path that runs above Deep Dale, affording an impressive view into the valley. After a while, turning a slight bend, the ruined church of the abandoned settlement comes spectacularly into sight. Just beyond that point, look for a waymark that directs the path on an angle down the slope, heading directly towards the church.

Through a kissing-gate at the bottom, carry on around a small pond to another gate into the churchyard. Leaving at the far side, walk past the site of the old vicarage to yet another gate beside a couple of mid-18th-century cottages.

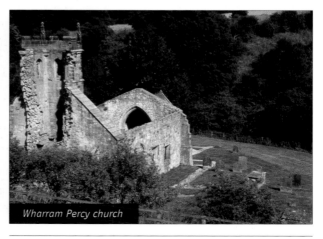

Wharram Percy church

Dropping into Wharram Percy

Beyond the cottages, the path rises between the foundations of an 18th-century farmstead to meet another path. Go right past grassy mounds, all that remains of the medieval cottages. At the bottom, leave through a gate and cross a track to a footbridge over a brook **C**.

Climb to the pasture above and bear right to another gate on the opposite side. Still following Yorkshire Wolds Way signs, the ongoing path ascends along the base of a narrow fold to return you to the car park. ●

Times gone by

Archaeological evidence shows settlement in the valley since Neolithic times, but it is during the medieval period that it peaked as a prosperous farming community. Mounds and hollows indicate the extent of the village cottages and gardens, while larger fields extended onto the wold. At the centre stood the church, the only building to survive after the last villagers were evicted early in the 16th century to make way for more profitable sheep walks. Until the church at Thixendale was opened in 1870, it continued to serve the surrounding dales, but then gradually fell out of use and finally closed in 1949.

SCALE 1:25000 or 2½ INCHES to 1 MILE 4CM to 1KM

Dunstanburgh Castle

Start
Craster

Distance
4¾ miles (7.6km)

Height gain
380 feet (115m)

Approximate time
2½ hours

Route terrain
Well used paths

Parking
Car park at edge of village

OS maps
Landrangers 75 (Berwick-upon-Tweed) and 81 (Alnwick & Morpeth), Explorer 332 (Alnwick & Amble)

GPS waypoints
NU 256 198
Ⓐ NU 257 213
Ⓑ NU 245 224
Ⓒ NU 250 207

Overlooking the North Sea, Dunstanburgh Castle is an evocative sight, with early morning mist or the long shadows of evening adding their own magical qualities. It is reached on foot from the picturesque hamlet of Craster, typical of the many villages along England's eastern coast that once derived a living from the sea. Although the fisheries have declined, the smokehouse still thrives and the aroma of kippers pervades the village.

Follow the road down to the harbour, there turning left past cottages. Through a gate at the end, a path continues above the sloping rocky shore towards the distant castle. The rocks trap countless pools from the receding tide, home to small crabs, shrimps and sea anemones. Immediately beyond the second gate Ⓐ, the path splits, that ahead leading to the castle entrance.

Castle defences

Begun around 1313 by Thomas, Earl of Lancaster, Dunstanburgh Castle sits imposingly upon an outcrop of the Great Whin Sill. This massive geological feature underlies the north Pennines and part of Hadrian's Wall, making a final appearance off the coast as the Farne Islands. The castle's curtain walls enclose some 9 acres, heightening the natural defences of the sea cliffs and steep inland bank that protect it on three sides. The entrance lies through an impressive gatehouse flanked by twin towers. The fortification remained impregnable until the Wars of the Roses, when it succumbed to the Earl of Warwick's pounding canon. Abandoned, it crumbled into a romantic ruin.

Return to the fork and go right, passing through a marshy depression beneath the western defences and the striking Lilburn Tower. Once open to the sea, the channel provided a harbour for Henry VIII's fleet in 1514. Rejoining the coast, pause to look back at the high cliffs protecting the castle's northern flank, which, in early summer, echo with the screams of countless nesting kittiwakes. Walk on past the Greymare Rock, a contorted, layered slab lying towards the head of the beach.

Keep above the shore past the golf course, the sand hills hiding a couple of pill boxes, part of the coastal defences during the last war. Eventually, the dunes are broken by a gap Ⓑ, through which a path runs from the beach across the golf

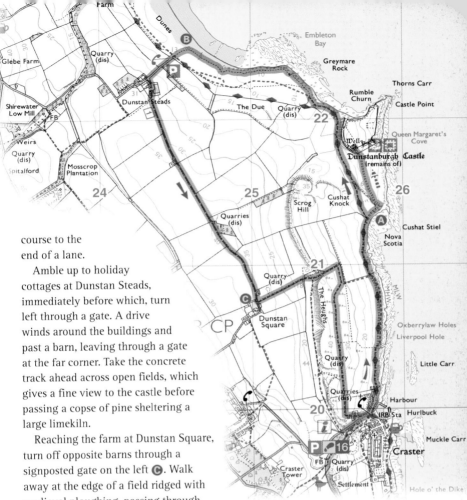

course to the end of a lane.

Amble up to holiday cottages at Dunstan Steads, immediately before which, turn left through a gate. A drive winds around the buildings and past a barn, leaving through a gate at the far corner. Take the concrete track ahead across open fields, which gives a fine view to the castle before passing a copse of pine sheltering a large limekiln.

Reaching the farm at Dunstan Square, turn off opposite barns through a signposted gate on the left Ⓒ. Walk away at the edge of a field ridged with medieval ploughing, passing through another gate at the bottom to climb to a nick in The Heughs, the line of cliffs ahead. At the top, keep the same line beside a fence to the corner. Go through the gate on the right and walk away with the fence. After passing by a second gate, bear off to take a parallel course some 50 yds to the right. Later joining another fence, carry on toward Craster's cottages, which now appear ahead. Over a stile, the ongoing path is contained by clumps of gorse behind the long gardens of the fishermen's cottages. At the end, swing left to meet a street, which falls into the village. The car park is then just a short distance to the right. ●

SCALE 1:25 000 or 2½ INCHES to 1 MILE 4CM to 1KM

Ancient past
The coast path south of the village past Cullernose Point and Rumbling Kern is dramatic too and leads past an area where an Iron Age camp and Bronze Age burials have been found. Even earlier are traces of a Mesolithic settlement, which, until recently, was the earliest known in Britain. A sufficiency of game, birds, fish and perhaps even seals might have encouraged them to settle, and a reconstructed hut above the shore, some 2½ miles south of the village portrays a simple dwelling.

walk 17

Start
Rievaulx Terrace

Distance
3¾ miles (6km)

Height gain
700 feet (210m)

Approximate time
2 hours

Route terrain
Clear tracks, paths and lane

Parking
Car parks at Helmsley then take seasonal bus to Rievaulx

OS maps
Landranger 100 (Malton & Pickering), Explorer OL 26 (North York Moors – Western Area)

GPS waypoints
- SE 582 852
- Ⓐ SE 579 840
- Ⓑ SE 583 835
- Ⓒ SE 595 835

Rievaulx and Helmsley

Parking is limited at Rievaulx, therefore leave your car in Helmsley and take the seasonal Moorsbus to Rievaulx Terrace. After visiting the terrace gardens and the abbey in the village below, follow the walk back to the town to see the sights there. When the bus is not operating, the distance is not so great as to preclude walking both there and back.

The entrance to Rievaulx Terrace lies beside the junction of the B1257 with the narrow lane to Rievaulx.

Affording stunning vistas over the Rye Valley and the abbey, the ½-mile terrace walk linking two 'temples' was created in 1758 by Thomas Duncombe of Duncombe Park near Helmsley. That approached first is in the Ionic style and was inspired by the Temple of Portunus in Rome. Complete with basement kitchens it was used as a banqueting hall. At the southern end is the circular Tuscan Temple, whose floor was said to have been taken from the abbey below.

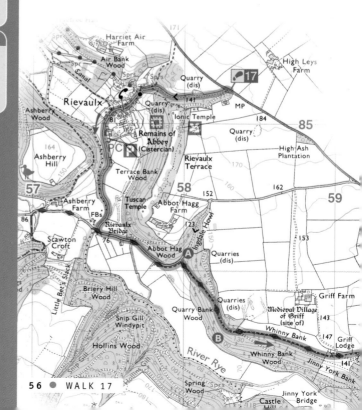

Rievaulx Abbey

Follow the lane downhill into the village, where you will find the entrance to Rievaulx Abbey on your left.

Rievaulx monastery

Begun in 1132, Rievaulx was the first Cistercian monastery in northern England and founded by 12 monks from Clairvaux in France. Led by an English abbot, William, they faced a daunting task in clearing woodland, draining marshes, diverting rivers and constructing canals and fishponds to tame the 'vast solitude and horror', which an early writer ascribed to the valley. It took over 100 years to complete the abbey church and its attendant buildings, which, at its peak, supported 140 monks and 600 lay brothers.

Continue along the lane, paralleling the River Rye downstream to Rievaulx Bridge. Turn left below Abbot Hag Wood, but just after the lane bends left into Ingdale Howl, take a woodland track on the right, signed to Helmsley **A**.

The way climbs steadily through Quarry Bank Wood, later levelling below disused quarry workings now almost hidden by lush vegetation. If not pressed for time, go left at a waymarked crossing track a little farther on **B**. It leads to a field, where grassy mounds and shallow ditches, once presumed to

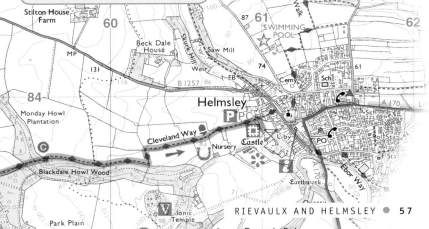

be an abandoned medieval village are now thought to mark the monastery's original grange.

Returning to **B**, continue with the main track, which runs at the edge of fields above Whinny Bank Wood. At the far end, carry on over open ground past Griff Lodge. Keep ahead across its drive on the continuation of the Cleveland Way. Eventually, after passing through consecutive gates, the route drops steeply into Blackdale Howl, climbing beyond to emerge at the edge of expansive fields **C**.

An enclosed path follows the perimeter, in due course turning to climb around the far end. Through a kissing-gate at the top, go right onto a developing track, which gradually descends towards Helmsley. The track ultimately ends by Helmsley's long-stay car park. Turn right to explore the castle and town, or carry on ahead to the end

> **Helmsley Castle** The 12th-century castle was built primarily for defence and has imposing earthwork embankments and a spectacular ruined keep. Inside, Tudor apartments contrast with the stark military architecture, and were built when comfort later assumed a greater precedence. However, when Thomas Duncombe inherited the estate, he desired more than a draughty old castle, and in 1713, began work on a fine new house. Having survived two disastrous fires and 60 years as a girls' school, it has been superbly restored by the Duncombe family and is open to the public.

of the street, where the 13th-century church lies to the right.

Brief route instructions from Helmsley
From the vehicle entrance to the long-stay car park, turn left along the Cleveland Way. Carry on at the field edge beyond the track's end to a kissing-gate, from which an enclosed path drops left and then runs above Blackdale Howl Wood. Entering trees **C** the path dips across a valley, emerging beyond and later crossing a drive by Griff Lodge. The Cleveland Way runs on ahead above Whinny Bank Wood, subsequently dropping through the trees and finally meeting a lane at the foot of Ingdale Howl **A**. Go left to Rievaulx Bridge and turn right to the abbey. Continue beyond up the hill to Rievaulx Terrace. ●

Helmsley Castle

Lindisfarne – a castle and a priory

An Irish monk, Saint Aidan, brought Christianity to the kingdom of Northumbria in 635, founding a monastery on Lindisfarne under the patronage of King Oswald from which to conduct his mission. Today, cut off twice a day by the tide, the tiny island remains an evocative place, rich in both wildlife and historical remains. There is much to see and it is worth spending the full day on the island.

Note: Consult tide tables to check safe crossing times.

From the northern end of the car park, walk back along the lane towards the shore. Leave through a signposted gate before the bend for a path at the edge of the dunes. Where it splits beyond the fields, keep ahead, passing the remains of a limekiln. Gaining height across the dunes, a view opens over the island. Maintain direction towards the northern coast, shortly encountering a ruin **A**. Pass it on the right to find a gap in a cattle fence and walk out to the shore.

Turn right behind a sandy beach, which soon gives way to the low rocky slabs of Back Skerrs. In places smooth, elsewhere fractured, eroded and littered with boulders, the wave-washed rocks are of carboniferous sandstone, shale and limestone, the strata gently undulating as if emulating the swell of the sea.

Saint Aidan

Aidan's purpose was to take Christianity to Northumbria, and coming from Iona, chose the seclusion of this island upon which to establish his monastic retreat. After 17 years as Bishop, Aidan died at Bamburgh and was later succeeded by Cuthbert, a young shepherd boy who had been inspired by a vision of Aidan's soul rising to heaven. Cuthbert was renowned for his piety and generosity to the poor, but in later life sought the solitude of the Farne Islands. While there, he decreed protection for the nesting eider ducks, which today are known locally as Cuddy Ducks. After his death in 687 he was interred at Lindisfarne, but when his casket was opened 11 years later, his corpse was found to be preserved and miracles were attributed to him. When the community abandoned the island in the face of raiding Vikings, they took his body with them. After many long years of wandering via Melrose, Chester-le-Street and Ripon, Cuthbert's body was finally laid to rest at Durham.

Start
Holy Island

Distance
5½ miles (8.9km)

Height gain
200 feet (60m)

Approximate time
3 hours

Route terrain
Coastal paths, rocky beaches and sand dunes

Parking
Car park at edge of village

OS maps
Landranger 75 (Berwick-upon-Tweed), Explorer 340 (Holy Island and Bamburgh)

GPS waypoints
NU 125 425
A NU 119 435
B NU 139 436
C NU 129 419
D NU 125 419

Hollows steal water from the receding tide wherein lurk tiny creatures, while barnacles and seaweeds coat the rocks. *Take care as it can be slippery underfoot.*

Rounding the point brings you to the small, sandy bay of Coves Haven, sheltered by low cliffs at the far side. At low tide you can pick your way across the boulders, but at high water you must resort to a path along the top. Beyond Castlehead Rocks is a much larger bay, split by the reef of Keel Head extending into the sea.

Abandon the shore for the dunes as you approach a pyramidal navigation marker on Emmanuel Head **Ⓑ**, exchanging views past Berwick to Scotland for a panorama to the south. A flashing lighthouse on Longstone marks the archipelago of the Farne Islands, while Bamburgh Castle and closer to, Lindisfarne Castle majestically perch on rocky outcrops.

Turning down the eastern coast, the going is easier on the grass above the bouldery apron of shore. Carry on over a stile and through a gate, the island's only lake lying over to the right. Known simply as The Lough, it attracts over-wintering waterfowl, particularly the pale-bellied brent goose. Eventually an elevated pathway curves toward the castle. It carried a tramway transporting limestone to a massive kiln on the left, well preserved and best seen from the bottom.

The fort

The impressive fort, perched upon a dramatic intrusion of whinstone, was built around 1540 to protect the harbour, a landing used by the king's troops sent to quell border uprisings. After the Union of the Crowns in 1603, its need diminished, although the guns remained until 1819. Had it not been for the publisher, Edward Hudson, it would today probably be no more than a ruin. He bought the castle in 1901 and commissioned his friend, Edwin Lutyens to create from it a comfortable house, which he used for summer holidays and house parties. Hudson sold it on 20 years later and in 1944, the merchant banker, Sir Edward de Stein gave it to the National Trust.

Paths pass either side of the castle mound, although the entrance lies on the seaward flank. Beyond, a track leads

Lindisfarne Castle overlooks The Harbour bay

around The Harbour bay towards the village. Fork left at a junction **C**, passing a collection of upturned boats that serve as fishermen's sheds. Approaching the jetty area, bear right in front of a large hut to find a path climbing onto the Heugh behind.

The path drops steeply from the far end, where a track curves up right past St Mary's Church. Turn in through the churchyard and leave by the northern gate, passing the Lindisfarne Priory

Museum where you can get tickets for the priory.

Carry on into the village centre and keep ahead at the crossroads **D** to return to the car park.

The Heugh

This is another grand viewpoint and a navigation beacon, coastguard lookout and war memorial all take advantage of its elevation. It overlooks both the priory and the low offshore island to which St Cuthbert retreated before withdrawing to Inner Farne. At low tide, you can walk out to the island, where there are the scant remains of an early chapel.

The Priory

The priory ruins date from its refoundation as a Benedictine house in the 11th century, when monks returned from Durham. It was only a small community and briefly prospered until the surrounding area was repeatedly harried during border unrest. The monastery was dissolved in 1537 under Henry VIII's decree.

SCALE 1:25 000 or 2½ INCHES to 1 MILE 4CM to 1KM

Castle Howard

Start

Welburn, by The Crown and Cushion

Distance

5½ miles (8.9km)

Height gain

420 feet (125m)

Approximate time

3 hours

Route terrain

Field paths and estate tracks

Parking

Roadside parking at Welburn

OS maps

Landranger 100 (Malton & Pickering), Explorer 300 (Howardian Hills & Malton)

GPS waypoints

- SE 720 680
- Ⓐ SE 722 692
- Ⓑ SE 719 706
- Ⓒ SE 732 694
- Ⓓ SE 730 687
- Ⓔ SE 723 679

Cradled within a fold of the Howardian Hills, Castle Howard is one of the finest Baroque mansions in England, but its full magnificence is only revealed within the setting of its wider landscape. Explored here are the park, woodland and lakes surrounding the house, where a temple summerhouse, whimsical follies and a grand mausoleum repeat the bold architectural experiment of the centrepiece across the estate.

With The Crown and Cushion on your left and the Barley Basket Tearoom on your right, walk along Main Road and take the first left down Water Lane. Bear left at the end through a barrier and continue along a track in the direction of Coneysthorpe. Keep ahead at a junction towards woodland, where the path enters the trees and falls to cross a stream. Climb away beyond, emerging through a gate at the top of the wood. Carry on to reach a tarmac track Ⓐ.

Go left but almost immediately, turn off right, heading down to New River Bridge, from which there is a good view

Charles Howard

Charles Howard, the third Earl of Carlisle began building in 1699, employing the then unproved architect Vanbrugh and his able assistant Hawksmoor, a protégé of Wren. A century and three generations of Carlisles passed before the hall was finally completed and its park landscaped and set with grandiose follies in the fashion of the era. From the ornate bridge, you can see the Pyramid and Temple, while to the east is a great mausoleum, where the third Earl was finally laid to rest.

Castle Howard

upstream to Castle Howard.

Climb away across the park over a rise, dropping on the far side to a three-way fingerpost by the corner of a fence. Still following signs to Coneysthorpe, go left joining a track beside a stone wall. Follow it through a gate into trees to a junction **B**.

Walk right, shortly crossing Mill Hills Beck before rising into more woodland and another junction by Bog Hall Farm. Signed right towards Gaterley, the ongoing track weaves left and right between the buildings to continue beyond at the edge of fields. Eventually reaching another farm at Low Gaterley, turn right in front of a barn and head uphill to reach a tarmac drive **C**.

Walk right for a little over ½ mile to meet your outward route at **A**. Briefly retrace your steps to the wood cloaking East Moor Banks. Go through the gate but now turn left at a signpost to Cranbeck, following a path that wanders within the trees along the top of the bank. After ½ mile, look for a path signed off to the right **D**. Just before a small clearing stands another of the estate's whimsical monuments, a pillar aptly called Four Faces.

The path descends through the trees to re-cross Moorhouse Beck. Over a stile, walk on to a junction and keep ahead on a bridleway, marked towards Welburn. Leaving the wood through a gate, carry on beside a field to another gate. Bear right with the bridleway, but at a fork, just a few yards farther on, branch right on a footpath, still following signs to Welburn. The trod strikes across rough pasture towards the distant spire of Welburn's church. At the far side, keep ahead through a gap along the edge of a field. Reaching the corner, take a left diagonal across a final field to emerge onto the lane at the edge of the village **E**. Turn right back to the starting point. ●

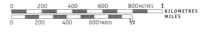

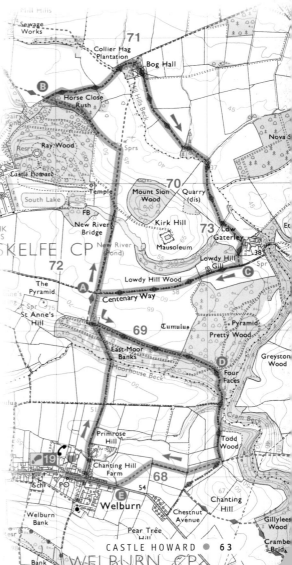

Start

Durham, Market Place

Distance

5½ miles (8.9km)

Height gain

650 feet (195m)

Approximate time

3 hours

Route terrain

Field and riverside paths

P Parking

Durham

OS maps

Landranger 88 (Newcastle upon Tyne), Explorer 308 (Durham & Sunderland)

GPS waypoints

🖉 NZ 273 425
Ⓐ NZ 275 424
Ⓑ NZ 286 418
Ⓒ NZ 287 410
Ⓓ NZ 284 416
Ⓔ NZ 277 407
Ⓕ NZ 274 415
Ⓖ NZ 274 431

The ancient city of Durham

Durham's history begins in 995 when St Cuthbert's relics were interred in a small chapel, ending a wandering journey that began 120 years earlier when monks fled Lindisfarne with his coffin. The present cathedral was founded late in the 11th century, replacing earlier chapels built to house his shrine, while the nearby castle was the seat of the powerful Prince Bishops. Together they symbolise the spiritual and military powers of the Prince Bishops of Durham.

After the Norman Conquest this corner was a buffer between England and the troublesome borderland straddling Northumbria and Scotland. The Prince Bishops, entrusted with the task of protecting the area from Scottish invasion, were endowed with almost regal powers and controlled their own parliament, court, army and coinage. In their castles at Durham and Bishop Auckland they lived like kings and it was not until 1536 that Henry VIII removed much of their secular power. Although altered and rebuilt, Durham Castle retains much of its original Norman design, the major changes coming after 1840 when it was given to the newly founded university and transformed into a residential college.

The Cathedral

Durham Cathedral is a masterpiece of Norman architecture, widely regarded as the finest in Europe. The main body was constructed between 1093 and 1133, although the east end and central tower date from the 13th century. Inside, soaring columns dominate the nave, each decorated with bold carvings. St Cuthbert's tomb, which stood at the eastern end of the building, was destroyed at the Dissolution. His body, which even then was found to have remained uncorrupted, was reburied beneath the floor. Other relics of the Cathedral include the head of St Oswald and the body of Bede, who is buried at the west end.

🖉 The walk starts in the Market Place. With your back to St Michael's Church, bear left along Saddler Street. At a fork take the left-hand, lower street to Elvet Bridge, descending steps on the left to the River Wear Ⓐ. Continue along the riverside path, passing beneath a modern road-bridge. Reaching a junction

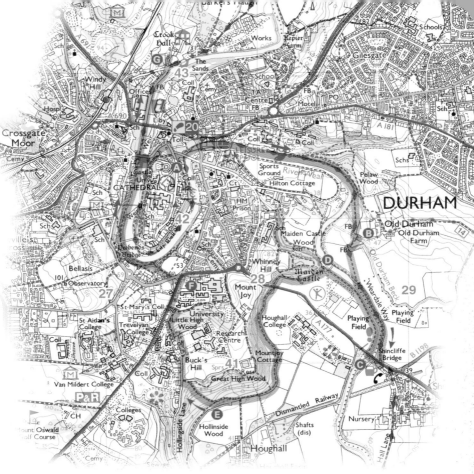

SCALE 1:25000 or 2½ INCHES to 1 MILE 4CM to 1KM

| 0 | 200 | 400 | 600 | 800 METRES | 1 |
| | 200 | 400 | 600 YARDS | ½ | KILOMETRES MILES |

bridge. Walk past and then bear left across the field corner to a kissing-gate into Maiden Castle Wood **D**. Turn left

opposite the City Boathouse, where the river bends right, leave the bank and keep ahead on the cycle track. After 400 yds, just round a left bend, turn right **B**, passing between the abutments of a demolished bridge. Carry on over a footbridge spanning Old Durham Beck and bear left across a playing field to rejoin the riverside. Continue upstream, eventually meeting a main road at the edge of Shincliffe opposite the Rose Tree Inn **C**.

Turn over Shincliffe Bridge and right again, following the river back down to Maiden Castle suspension

Durham Market Place

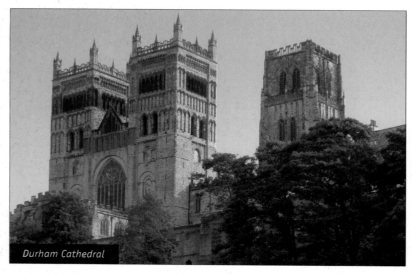

Durham Cathedral

around the base of the thickly wooded hill, on top of which was Maiden Castle, a prehistoric fort. At a fork, keep left, the way curving back to the main road.

Cross to the path opposite, which runs within the edge of Great High Wood, a delightful part of the walk with pleasant views across fields to the left. At a fork by a bench **E**, keep right up a steepening path. Bear left at the top, crossing a stile onto a lane. Turn right, passing the entrance to the Durham University Botanic Gardens on your left.

Follow the lane into the university campus. As it bends left in front of the Victor Watts Library building, turn right along the descending lane. Walk beside a hall of residence and continue downhill, bearing right to pass to the right of a tennis court. At the foot of steps, go left to the main road. Cross and head right to a major crossroads **F**, there swinging left along Quarry Heads Lane. A short way along, take a footpath on the right, which passes the edge of a playing field and then drops through woodland to a fork.

Take the right-hand branch, which bends left to join the riverside. The final section through woods beside the River Wear takes you past Prebends Bridge and below Durham Cathedral and Castle to Framwellgate Bridge. Equally unmissable is Crook Hall, a fine medieval house set in beautifully restored gardens. Carry on beside the river for another ½ mile, joining the adjacent lane to find the entrance on the left **G**. Return to cross Framwellgate Bridge, following Silver Street back to the Market Place. ●

St Cuthbert

The foundation of the city is illustrated by a carving on the south side of the cathedral. According to legend, monks returning St Cuthbert's body to Chester-le-Street after it had been removed to Ripon to ensure its safety from Viking raiders, arrived at Warden Law, when miraculously, the coffin would move no further. Saint Cuthbert appeared in a vision, pronouncing that his body should be taken to Dun Holm. But no one knew where that was until they encountered a milkmaid on her way there to search for her lost cow. The monks now found that they could pick up the bier and followed her to the place, a wooded promontory overlooking a looping gorge of the Wear.

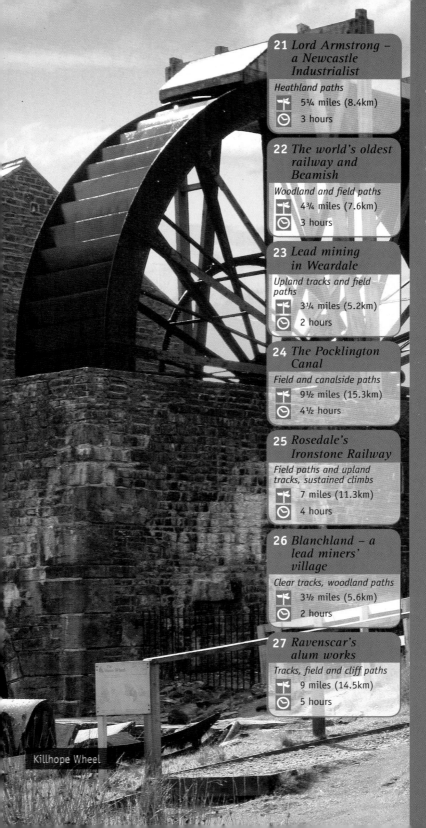

Killhope Wheel

Industrial Heritage

Industrial Heritage

A wooden coal wagon

Numerous places stake claim to being a cradle of industrialisation, and that of north eastern England is as valid as many. Copper, silver and iron ores were already being dug from the Pennine Hills when the Romans arrived in Britain and, here at the northernmost outpost of their empire, they mined iron ore and coal near the mouth of the Tees and lead ore around Alston. While the workings were largely abandoned after they left, the dawn following the Dark Ages brought a new interest in the region's mineral resources; the coal and iron deposits of Northumberland and Durham, the veins of lead in the Pennines and iron ore beneath the North York Moors. Ports sprang up at the river estuaries, with Newcastle exporting wool, coal, stone, glass and a host of other products, while Kingston on the River Hull was the focus of navigable access to a rich agricultural hinterland.

A major industry that developed during the 17th century was the production of alum, a chemical vital to the tanning and dyeing industries. Throughout the Middle Ages its production was a papal monopoly and the process of its extraction a closely guarded secret. In 1595, Sir Thomas Challoner of Guisborough discovered alum-bearing shales in the Cleveland Hills and smuggled workers from Italy to establish his own business. Alum shale outcrops in many locations around the North York Moors, and at Peak on the east coast, since renamed **Ravenscar**, the workings and processing buildings can be seen. The industry boomed until the middle of the 19th century, when a simpler process utilising colliery waste was discovered.

Besides raw materials, the Industrial Revolution required both power and effective transport, so it is not surprising that the first factory towns grew beside fast flowing streams and navigable river systems or coastal ports. Elsewhere, navigations and canals brought new opportunities by providing fast and cost effective transport, but the impossibly hilly terrain of north eastern England generally rendered such enterprise impractical. The only one to be built within this region was the **Pocklington Canal** on the edge of the Yorkshire Wolds, which created access to the Vale of York's navigable rivers.

The real impetus for the region came with the development of the railways, without which its iron industry would never have emerged. Horse-drawn, wooden-railed wagonways had been used to service coal mines above Newcastle from the 17th century and the Tanfield

Railway claims to be the oldest working railway in the world. And although no longer used, the **Causey Arch** beside it is the world's oldest railway bridge. Close by is the **Beamish museum**, which recreates many aspects of northern life at two important periods of its history a century apart.

Another of the region's early railroads is the North York Moors Railway, surveyed by George Stephenson and opened in 1836. It too was originally horse-drawn and ran from Pickering to the seaport of Whitby, carrying both passengers and freight. Now restored, it is one of the most scenic lines in the country. Designed purely as a mineral railway, the Rosedale branch of the North York and Cleveland Railway began operating in 1858, the **Ironstone Railway**. Running across the remote, high moors, its construction and operation presented significant difficulties, not least being the 700-foot difference in altitude between the moor and the valley. The two levels were connected via a mile-long 1 in 5 incline, which used the weight of descending full wagons to haul empty ones back to the summit.

Weardale's mining and quarrying industries were also serviced by a railway, which reached Wearhead in 1895. However, lead mining had already operated on an industrial scale for over a century, exploiting rich veins of ore. The area around Cowshill was particularly productive throughout the 19th century and the hillsides are littered with shafts, spoil heaps and hushes. Packhorses were used to carry out the ore and metal

before the railway, but shortly after its arrival, falling prices took the industry into decline. The Killhope Lead Mining Museum, a little higher up the valley paints a vivid picture of how the ore was mined and processed.

Limestone was another important product of Weardale. As well as making mortar for building, it was necessary for the smelting of iron ore. From the 18th century, slaked lime was also widely used to improve the fertility of land and right across the country you will come across the ruins of small limekilns where the stone was burnt.

From the 16th century, Newcastle grew rich on the back of coal. But shipbuilding was also important and, as the industrial era gathered pace, it developed as one of the world's heavy engineering capitals. The greatest of the city's industrialists to emerge during the 19th century was **William Armstrong**. Entrepreneur and practical inventor, he abandoned a career in law for engineering and, following the success of his design for a hydraulic crane for the Newcastle Docks, he established his own company at Elswick. He subsequently branched into bridge building, armaments and eventually warships. Armstrong's country house at **Cragside** is not only an elegant Victorian home, but also full of ingenious domestic applications for his inventions. Water power was used to provide electricity for lighting and a telephone system as well as operating a lift and a mechanical roasting spit.

walk 21

Start
Rothbury

Distance
5¼ miles (8.4km)

Height gain
830 feet (250m)

Approximate time
3 hours

Route terrain
Heathland paths

P Parking
Beggars Rigg car park, ¼ mile west of Rothbury along B6341

OS maps
Landranger 81 (Alnwick & Morpeth), Explorer 332 Alnwick & Amble)

GPS waypoints
- NU 050 015
- Ⓐ NU 046 017
- Ⓑ NU 046 020
- Ⓒ NU 046 032
- Ⓓ NU 060 033
- Ⓔ NU 056 032
- Ⓕ NU 054 024

Lord Armstrong – a Newcastle Industrialist

Rothbury clusters around a bridge over the River Coquet, its attractive setting belying a troubled past during the centuries of border unrest. The sandstone hills to the north explored on the walk formed part of the Victorian country estate of Lord Armstrong. His house, Cragside, now looked after by the National Trust, is off the B6341, a short drive to the north east and well worth a visit.

Leave the car park past a viewing platform to reach the road above. Follow it towards the town, turning sharp left opposite Rothbury House, which opened in 1789 as a private hotel. Head up the hill, continuing for another 400 yds after it levels to find steps set into the wall on the right beside the entrance drive of 'Midmar' Ⓐ. A path runs between the houses, curving left to tackle the steep wooded bank behind.

Reaching the top, mount a ladder-stile at the end of a wall. Keep ahead below an outcrop before passing into open pasture. Instead of going through the gate behind the cottage, Gimmerknowe, turn right and follow a developing grass track beside the wall. Meeting a gravel track Ⓑ, turn left along it, later passing a house, Whinhams at Brae Head.

Rising beyond, the track curves to join a wall. After passing a gate at the end of Physic Lane, track and wall diverge. Keep

Armstrong's grand country house, Cragside

Born at Newcastle in 1810, William George Armstrong began his professional life as a solicitor. But his real interest lay in engineering, and his early work centred on hydraulics and electricity generation. After designing a crane for use in the shipyards he opened his own factory in 1847. Armstrong then focussed his work on bridge construction and armaments and was knighted for his design of an accurate breech-loading field gun. He subsequently turned to the manufacture of naval guns and then warships. In 1863, Armstrong began building Cragside above Rothbury, a place he had often visited as a child. He later restored the castle at Bamburgh and was a great benefactor to his own city, Newcastle, founding the origins of the university and supporting the building of the Hancock Museum.

shallow rise to intersect a more pronounced crossing track **C**.

Go left, the way soon bending around to the north east and drawing beside a stone wall. After briefly following its course, the track moves into woodland. Shortly reaching a crossing track, go through the field gate opposite, the way signed to Primrose Cottage. The trail gently descends at the edge of the wood overlooking a picturesque valley.

At Primrose Cottage **D**, turn right through a gate into Primrose Wood. Climb away for ¼ mile to a junction

going past a clump of trees behind another short section of wall and, where the track then forks, take the left branch. Carry on across the heather moor over a

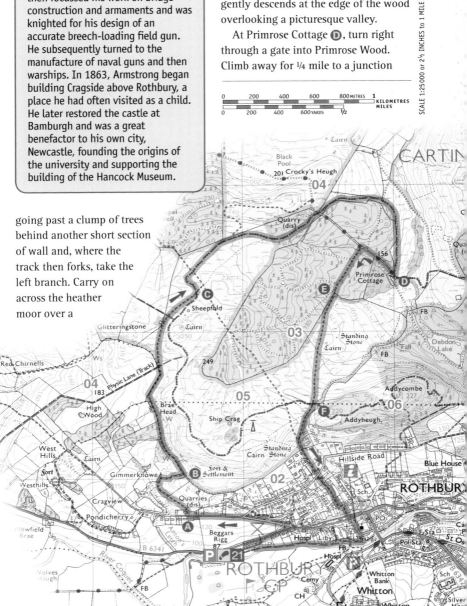

SCALE 1:25000 or 2½ INCHES to 1 MILE 4CM to 1KM

One of Armstrong's water wheels

where Rothbury is signed left. Undulate through the trees for another ¼ mile, then, just beyond a junction on the right, look for a narrow path bearing down left to a small gate **E**. A clear path leads away over a footbridge across an expanse of sandy heath. Beyond a boggy stream, it rises to meet a stony track emerging from Addyheugh Wood **F**.

Cross to the continuing path opposite, which follows the forest fence. After a few yards, you can deviate onto the hill for the fine panorama across the Coquet valley to the Simonside Hills. Return to the path and wander downhill at the edge of the forest, eventually reaching a stile off the heath.

A contained path drops between house gardens to a street. Carry on downhill to a junction. Turn right and almost immediately left to pick up another path. At the bottom of that, go left and right along a final passageway that ends in the centre of Rothbury.

Cross to the street opposite and walk down past the church. Where it bends sharply left, keep ahead along a path beside the old Haa-Hill burial ground.

Drop to a riverside path and follow it upstream. Reaching the picnic area, climb the bank to the car park above. ●

Haa-Hill burial ground

It occupies the site of Rothbury Castle, which apparently remained occupied until the 1850s but then became ruinous and was pulled down to create extra burial space for the parish. The graveyard contains a number of noteworthy memorials, including the Armstrong family tomb.

The world's oldest railway and Beamish

This enjoyable wander through the gorges and woodlands around Causey links three of the North East's great industrial and social heritage sites, Causey Arch, the Tanfield Railway and the Beamish North of England Open Air Museum. The entrances to the railway (East Tanfield Station) and the museum lie only a short drive away from the start of the walk.

 Begin by a railway bridge at the southern exit of the car park, along a path signposted right to Causey Arch. It descends gently through trees beside the railway embankment. At a fork, bear right and continue down into the gorge. Ignore the first footbridge over Causey Burn and instead turn left alongside the stream to cross at a second footbridge.

Carry on through the wooded gorge, re-crossing the burn at the next footbridge. Climb steps and turn right, the Causey Arch coming into view at the next bend. Cross the burn yet again and go on to the foot of the splendid arch, from which steps climb beside the abutment to the bridge **A**.

> **Causey Arch**   Completed in 1726, for 30 years it remained the longest single-span bridge in the country. It was built across the Causey Gorge as part of a wagonway to transport coal from the Tanfield coal-fields to boats waiting on the Tyne. It was an immediate success and for a time, over 900 tubs of coal were hauled across every day. But after a few years, the smaller mines became worked out and in 1740 a disastrous fire closed the main Tanfield Colliery. Despite the relatively short period during which the bridge was fully used, it was a bold experiment in structural engineering and the 150-foot span taking the track 80 feet above the river was a tremendous achievement.

Walk across to see a reconstruction of a coal tub and the track on which it ran, and then go a short distance to the right to enjoy a superb view back to the bridge.

Go back over the bridge and carry on ahead through the woods. Keep left at a fork on a path along the top of the Causey Gorge, later gradually descending to a bridge **B**. Cross and go

Start
Beamish Country Park off A6076, 4 miles southwest of Gateshead

Distance
4¾ miles (7.6km)

Height gain
800 feet (245m)

Approximate time
3 hours

Route terrain
Woodland and field paths

Parking
Causey Arch Picnic Area

OS maps
Landranger 88 (Newcastle upon Tyne), Explorer 308 (Durham & Sunderland)

GPS waypoints
- NZ 204 561
- **A** NZ 201 558
- **B** NZ 195 551
- **C** NZ 205 552
- **D** NZ 204 546
- **E** NZ 215 542
- **F** NZ 211 549
- **G** NZ 207 561

The Causey Arch

left, the path rising from the wooded valley to a waypoint. Through gates, cross the Tanfield Railway and climb steps at the far side, curling with the path to a stile. Head uphill at the field edge, passing through a fence gap at the crest to continue down through immature woodland. At the bottom, a grass track leads left to the main road.

Cross and go down steps, turning right and then left over a stile. Walk down at the field edge to another stile in the corner. Head left to a gap between a wall and hedge and fork right, dropping beside woodland before entering the trees and descending steps to a footbridge beyond a clearing. At a fork keep left to a stile below electricity cables and then climb steeply beside a holly hedge to emerge on Beamishburn Road **C**.

Walk downhill, crossing Beamish Burn. About 200 yds beyond, turn left through an archway **D** and go ahead into the woods. After 30 yds fork right along a wider track, crossing a culvert and heading gently uphill. Beyond a wooden barrier, at a T-junction go left, subsequently forking left on a rising track beside the parkland wall and finally passing through a gap-stile onto Beamish Park Golf Course.

Head out past the eighth tee, beside a line of silver birch and then along a

grassy road towards Beamish Home Farm. There, to the right, a sign indicates the exit from the public footpath, climbing steps through the wall into a yard. Through a gate on the right, turn left through the period farmyard to a lane **E**.

Rail and coal

The Tyneside colliery owners had begun using tramways as an effective means of transporting coal in the middle of the 17th century, using wooden rails and tubs. The construction of the bridge represented a dramatic step forward, allowing direct access to the Tanfield collieries. Horses hauled the tubs up to Sunniside and were then re-harnessed behind to act as a brake as gravity took them down to the Tyne. Twin tracks were installed so that empty tubs could be taken back for re-filling. However, wooden rails soon wore out and braking friction could cause a fire, and eventually in 1839, the rails were replaced with iron. The railway was converted to steam in 1881 and although some passenger services were operated, it primarily serviced the collieries until its eventual closure in 1964. Part of the line was subsequently acquired by the Tanfield Railway, which now operates steam-hauled trains between East Tanfield and Sunniside, stopping at Causey Arch.

Follow the lane left past the grounds of the Beamish museum. Some 200 yds beyond a sharp left-hand bend, leave along Coppy Lane, a broad track on the right signed to Causey Arch **F**. Climbing steeply, pass through Coppy Wood, exiting beside a gate at the far side along a rough track between fields. Reaching a farm storage complex, fork right along a narrower path, which soon joins a drive out to a road **G**.

A restored shunter from the ironworks

Beamish museum

No trip to the area would be complete without a visit to the living museum at Beamish, where the life of the North East during the Victorian and later Georgian eras is vividly recreated. From the emergent railways to life on the farm, inside the squire's house to a colliery village and even the streets of a north eastern market town, faithfully reproduced to reflect the period just before the First World War.

The Causey Arch Inn is just 150 yds to the right, but the way back is to the left. A short way along, cross to a stile and head gently downhill at the field edge to emerge onto the main road. The tarmac drive opposite passes beneath a railway bridge to the car park. ●

Lead mining in Weardale

Start
Cowshill

Distance
3¼ miles (5.2km)

Height gain
775 feet (235m)

Approximate time
2 hours

Route terrain
Upland tracks and field paths

Parking
Car park by bridge at eastern end of village

OS maps
Landrangers 87 (Hexham & Haltwhistle) and 92 (Barnard Castle & Richmond), Explorer OL31 (North Pennines)

GPS waypoints
NY 856 406
Ⓐ NY 859 411
Ⓑ NY 868 407
Ⓒ NY 863 397
Ⓓ NY 857 396
Ⓔ NY 853 405

Cutting a deep furrow into the bleak uplands of the Northern Pennines, Weardale has been exploited for its minerals since at least the 12th century. By far the most important product was lead, but silver, iron and later fluorspar were also mined, while limestone, sandstone and whinstone were quarried. The lead industry peaked during the 1800s, drawing an influx of miners from other parts of the country. But towards the end of the century, lead prices began to fall causing the gradual closure of the mines and by the end of the First World War, the industry had all but finished.

Mining history

Almost 100 years have passed since the mines closed, but the hillsides still bear the vivid scars of hushes, shafts and spoil-heaps. Nowhere is the old industry and the conditions under which the miners, their children and womenfolk worked more vividly portrayed than at the Killhope Lead Mining Museum, which stands at the head of the valley. Guided underground tours, displays, reconstructions and demonstrations show how the ore was dug and processed, while a magnificently restored waterwheel powers some of the machinery once used. A nature trail leads through the woods on the hill behind, where reservoirs collected water to power the machinery. Red squirrels, birds, dragonflies and frogs are just some of the wildlife to be seen. A short way from Cowshill in the other direction is Irehopeburn, where the superb little Weardale Museum, located within High House Chapel, the oldest purpose-built Methodist chapel in continuous use, tells of home life within the valley.

Follow the track beyond the car park through a gate up into the valley enclosing Sedling Burn.

Higher up at a fork where the main track swings left over a bridge, bear right, climbing past the fenced enclosure of an old shaft over to the left to find a gate and signpost on the right Ⓐ. A bridle-track winds up the hill beside the gully of a stream. Carry on through another gate higher up, the track following workings that trace the line of the Sedling Vein. Eventually the climb levels as the track passes through a final gate beside more disused shafts Ⓑ.

Immediately abandon the track, turning right to a field gate. Head downhill at the edge of rough grazing with a wall on your right, curving around to a gate in the bottom corner. Continue your descent, the wall now on your left. Leaving through another gate bend right before a cottage, Halliwell House, a track then developing that falls downhill to meet a narrow lane.

Walk right, passing a cottage and then turn off beside it through a squeeze stile ⓒ. Head out of the corner, being drawn into a grassy fold that drops to a gate. Continue downhill past the grassy hillocks of more

An abandoned lead mine

grassed-over mine workings. At the bottom, a metalled track passes a cottage and winds into the hamlet of Wearhead.

Follow the main road right for 100 yds before turning left along a narrow lane signed to Wearhead Primary School ⓓ. After crossing a bridge over the River Wear, go through a gate on the right from which a field path is signed as the Weardale Way.

The trod meanders beside the river

from meadow to meadow, eventually passing through a kissing-gate in a wall near a stone barn. Bear left from the river, climbing a grassy bank and continue along the top of the bank

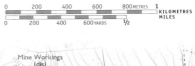

beside a wall on your left. At the far end, overlooking a small but impressive waterfall, which unfortunately is largely concealed by trees, swing through the wall to join a track that leads out to a lane. Go right, dropping to a bridge back across the river.

Just over the bridge, take a track on the right **E**, which wanders past a former mill. As it then swings right to cross a bridge over a side-stream, Sedling Burn, bear off left in front of a small terrace of cottages. Just beyond the last house, a stepped path climbs to the road in front of the Cowshill Hotel. Go right over the bridge and then immediately left back to the car park. ●

Lead ore

The abandonment of old mines near Sedling Burn is a mix of grassed-over heaps of spoil and rubble, fenced off pit shafts and the collapsed entrances to adits; horizontal tunnels that followed seams of lead ore into the hill. Rising to the left is Burtree Pasture, where the largest lead mine in the valley followed a rich vein 1,000 feet below the hill. The recovered ore was crushed and sorted to remove waste rock and then transported by packhorse to smelt mills at Rookhope, 6 miles away over the hill. Many of the old trails once used by the drovers still exist and have been incorporated within the footpath network.

Looking for lead ore

The Pocklington Canal

Pocklington prospered as a market town during the medieval period, trading in wool, livestock and grain, with a thriving brewing industry later developing. Its imposing church is locally known as the Cathedral of the Wolds, and has a Saxon foundation. The early Christian missionary Paulinus passed by in 627 on his way to York with King Edwin, and baptised villagers in the nearby beck. This is a longer, but easy walk exploring the pleasant countryside on the fringe of the Wolds and taking in a delightful stretch of canal.

walk 24

Start
Pocklington

Distance
9½ miles (15.3km)

Height gain
120 feet (35m)

Approximate time
4½ hours

Route terrain
Field and canalside paths

Parking
Pocklington

OS maps
Landranger 106 (Market Weighton), Explorer 294 (Market Weighton & Yorkshire Wolds Central)

GPS waypoints
SE 802 489
Ⓐ SE 798 482
Ⓑ SE 799 473
Ⓒ SE 785 452
Ⓓ SE 775 448
Ⓔ SE 757 453
Ⓕ SE 754 467
Ⓖ SE 783 473
Ⓗ SE 792 477

From the lower end of Market Place, walk along Railway Street, crossing a mini roundabout to leave town towards York. After ½ mile, turn left into Canal Lane Ⓐ. Reaching the main road, go left to the Wellington Oak and carefully cross to the Canal Head car park opposite Ⓑ. Picking up the towpath beside the basin, walk through a gate by Lock House and continue with the canal for 1¾ miles to Coat's Bridge Ⓒ.

Canal history

The suggestion of a canal giving access to the Humber Estuary had been mooted in the latter part of the 18th century, but work only began in 1815. It took three years to construct, but was one of Britain's few canal projects to be completed within budget. It connected Pocklington with the River Derwent at East Cottingwith, thus creating a navigable route to the Ouse at Barmby on the Marsh. Some 9½ miles long, the canal brought coal and lime to Pocklington, the returning barges taking farm produce to the industrial towns. However the canal never fully realised its potential, the railway, built in 1847, taking much of the trade. After the waterway closed in 1932, it fell into dereliction, but from 1969, progressive restoration of the locks has since opened the lower reaches to traffic, while the upper section is a splendid haven for wildlife, attracting birds such as coots, moorhens and swans.

Leave the canal and take the lane to the right. At the end, go left and then at the next junction Ⓓ right, following signs towards Thornton. Keep ahead for a mile into the village, continuing with the main lane beyond as it curves towards Sutton on Derwent Ⓔ. Carry on for a further mile to find a track on the right, just past a farm and marked as a footpath Ⓕ.

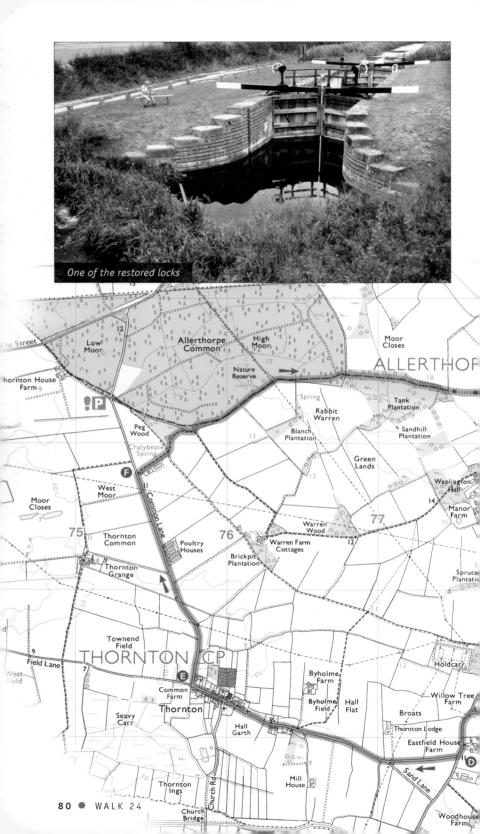

One of the restored locks

It heads away at the field margin towards trees. Swing left in front of a barn and then right to continue beside Allerthorpe Common. Where the track subsequently veers away, look for a kissing-gate into the wood. Walk through to a junction and take the obvious path to the right. It runs within the fringe of the common for over ½ mile before passing out through a gate

SCALE 1:25000 or 2½ INCHES to 1 MILE 4CM to 1KM

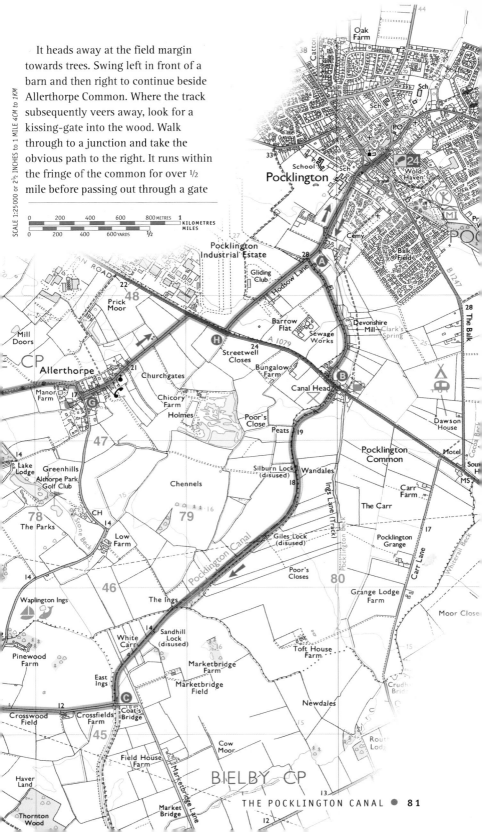

into the adjoining Tank Plantation. Eventually leaving the trees, the path merges with a track, which to the right leads past Manor Farm. Becoming a street, it swings right to meet the main lane in Allerthorpe beside the Plough Inn **G**.

Head left through the village, and on to the main road. Again, exercise caution in crossing to find a pavement on the far side, and walk right a short distance before abandoning it along Hodsow Lane **H**. Follow it back into Pocklington, less than a mile away. ●

The Pocklington Canal

Rosedale's Ironstone Railway

Walking through Rosedale today, it is difficult to imagine that this lovely, peaceful valley surrounded by empty moorland was once a busy iron-mining area that helped fuel the industries of Teesside. Mining and smelting began in the Middle Ages, when Byland Abbey was granted mineral rights in Rosedale. The industry climaxed in the 19th century, when the dale's population soared to nearly 3,000. Such a dramatic expansion was only made possible by the construction of a railway, which carried the ore across the bleak moors to Bloworth Crossing. Beyond there, it was lowered down Greenhow Bank via the Ingleby Incline to continue its journey to the furnaces of Middlesbrough. Only vestiges of the industry remain; ruinous pitheads, ironworkers' cottages and, above all, the route of the Ironstone Railway itself, poignant reminders of the area's intensively industrial past.

	Start
	Rosedale Abbey

	Distance
	7 miles (11.3km)

	Height gain
	1,050 feet (320m)

	Approximate time
	4 hours

	Route terrain
	Field paths and upland tracks, sustained climbs

	Parking
	Car park at start

	OS maps
	Landrangers 94 (Whitby & Esk Dale) and 100 (Malton & Pickering), Explorer OL26 (North York Moors - Western area)

	GPS waypoints
	SE 724 959
A	SE 710 967
B	SE 708 975
C	SE 692 971
D	SE 719 951

Walk away from the crossroads in the village centre with the green on your left. Turn right immediately beyond the school, skirting around it to then pass another small green just west of the church. Tucked away is a ruined tower, the only surviving fragment of the priory buildings. Just past there, immediately after a cottage on the left, the Old Police House, climb a wall stile and walk behind to a tarmac drive. Follow that right through a caravan site, leaving towards its far end through a gate to the right that takes the right of way into the corner of a field. Carry on beside the left-hand hedge, keeping the same direction beyond its eventual end. Through a gate, continue along the wooded banks of the River Seven.

> **Rosedale Abbey** Since the closure of the mines and railway in 1928, Rosedale Abbey has become a sparsely populated backwater, but popular with walkers. Of the 12th-century Cistercian nunnery, virtually nothing remains except for a small turret near the western end of the village church, the rest of the stone being plundered for the later building of the village.

Ignore a footbridge and then bear left at a junction immediately beyond to remain by the river. After negotiating another gate, walk ahead across successive fields, ultimately exiting through a gate onto a rough track. Follow it down left to cross a side stream and continue beside a fence to a stile. Cross and carry on through a gate beside the river once more, walking upstream as far as a footbridge **A**. Again do not cross, instead turn right along a paved way to a stile and ditch bridge in the top hedge. Continue climbing up the centre of the next two fields to a kissing-gate at the top. Through that, a track takes the way on at the field edge, finally emerging past a house onto a lane at Hill Cottages **B**.

Follow it left past the Ebenezer Methodist Church and Field Centre, but after a cottage just beyond, turn left down a drive to Craven Garth Cottages. Keep going through the farmyard to a gate and continue downhill at the field edge. Beyond the bottom of the second field, drop left down a bank to find a footbridge over the River Seven. On the far bank, climb left beside a fence, crossing stiles either side of a farm track to carry on up the hillside ahead. Over another stile by the left-hand of two gates at the top corner of that field, bear left to a marker and then keep ahead to reach a ladder-stile. Across that, walk ahead for 50 yds, but

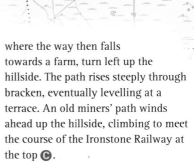

where the way then falls towards a farm, turn left up the hillside. The path rises steeply through bracken, eventually levelling at a terrace. An old miners' path winds ahead up the hillside, climbing to meet the course of the Ironstone Railway at the top **C**.

The way lies to the left, a superb, high-level walk of 2½ miles that passes some of the abandoned mine workings and offers an outstanding panorama across the Rosedale valley. There is a particularly impressive view where the track curves left above a steep, wooded bank high above the village and, on a clear day, you can see the pyramid-shaped buildings of the Fylingdale early warning station on the distant horizon.

Shortly, after passing through a barrier, the way divides at a fork **D**.

Calcining kilns

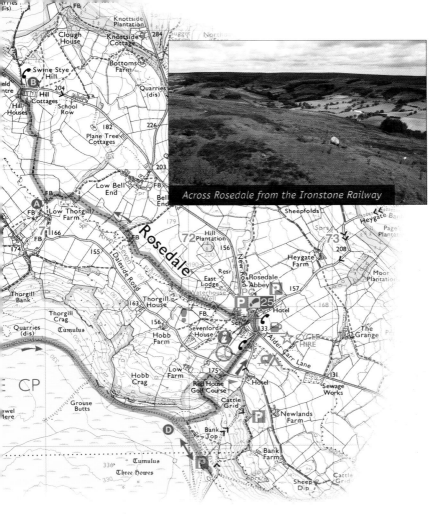

Across Rosedale from the Ironstone Railway

Walk ahead a little farther to see the kilns beyond Bank Top, where the iron ore was roasted to remove impurities before it was taken to the smelt furnaces at Middlesbrough.

Return to **D** and now turn sharp right below the main track. After 100 yds, where the trail then bends right towards a house, turn off left and follow a vague grass track straight down the hillside. Approaching a fence at the bottom, go left once more, dropping beside it to a stile. Keep walking downhill by a fence and broken wall, the path steepening as it approaches a ladder-stile. Carry on to a second ladder-stile on the right, which leads onto a golf course. Now, follow waymarks ahead and then left around the small clubhouse, continuing past it to leave by a stile below some trees. Cross a lane to another stile opposite and follow the descending field edge towards the village. Just before the bottom corner, cross a stile behind a cottage and drop beside it to emerge through its front gate onto the corner of a lane. Walk ahead to a junction and go left back into Rosedale Abbey. ●

SCALE 1:26 316 or 2½ INCHES to 1 MILE 3.8CM to 1KM

Blanchland – a lead miners' village

Start
Blanchland

Distance
3½ miles (5.6km)

Height gain
530 feet (160m)

Approximate time
2 hours

Route terrain
Clear tracks, woodland paths

Parking
Car park in village

OS maps
Landranger 87 (Hexham & Haltwhistle), Explorers OL43 (Hadrian's Wall - Haltwhistle & Hexham) and 307 (Consett & Derwent Reservoir)

GPS waypoints
NY 964 504
Ⓐ NY 963 509
Ⓑ NY 949 517
Ⓒ NY 958 499

Despite many preconceptions, the north of England has its fair share of unspoiled towns and villages, and few would disagree with Blanchland's claim to being one of the most picturesque. It nestles in a lovely wooded fold amid the bleak moors of the North Pennines AONB, a superb beginning for this fine walk connecting the sheltered valleys of Shildon Burn and the upper River Derwent.

In the beginning

Blanchland was founded in 1165 for the Premonstratensian order, originally as a priory, but later elevated under the rule of an abbot. It was from the White Canons that the place derived its name. Ever only a small community set amidst wild surroundings, life in the abbey appears to have been fairly austere and disrupted from time to time by border raiders. Local tales tell of one marauding band that became disoriented by the moorland mist and bypassed the abbey. But, the monks, in an over-eager celebration of their deliverance rang the bells, bringing back the raiders who were, unfortunately, still wandering about within earshot. Despite a short reprieve because of its usefulness as a hostel for travellers in this remote corner, the abbey was dissolved in 1539. The church was adapted for parish services and the guests' lodgings taken as a manor house. Lord Crew, Bishop of Durham, bought the estate in 1704, and is remembered in the name of the village pub, fittingly set within what remains of the old abbey guesthouse. On his death, he included the estate within a charitable trust and his trustees built the village we see today to house the lead miners.

Out of the car park, turn right but then almost at once go left and left again onto a rising track that is signed as a footpath. After climbing at the backs of cottages it swings into the woods behind the village. Ignore a path shortly branching off right and keep ahead up a sunken track to join a broader, green trail.

Descending gently to the left, watch for a waymarked path leaving on the right Ⓐ. Where it immediately splits, take the left branch, passing out of the trees through a small gate. Walk away above the wood at the edge of rough grazing, dropping at the far end into a leafy corner, where humps and hollows betray abandoned lead mines. Leaving at a gate, continue along a green track. Keep right through a gate in front of a cottage and

> **Mining** Lead has been mined in the area since at least medieval times, evidenced by the numerous hollows of collapsed bell pits in the area. During the 19th century, the improved techniques of the Industrial Age allowed deeper mining. The ruins beside the burn at Shildon centre on an engine house from this period, which was used for pumping water from the lower levels. The farm at the top of the hill apparently got its name from selling penny pies to miners walking to their work.

Old workings below Pennypie House

follow a track out to the end of a lane.

The route lies to the right, passing several of the old mine shafts fenced off in the trees on its way to Pennypie House, ¾ mile up the hill. As the track swings up to the farm, keep ahead through a gate **B** onto the open moor, but then immediately turn left across a bridge spanning the burn, the way signed to Baybridge.

A sandy track hugs the wall at the edge of the heather moor and gives good views across the head of the Derwent valley for the next ¾ mile. Eventually joining a track from a

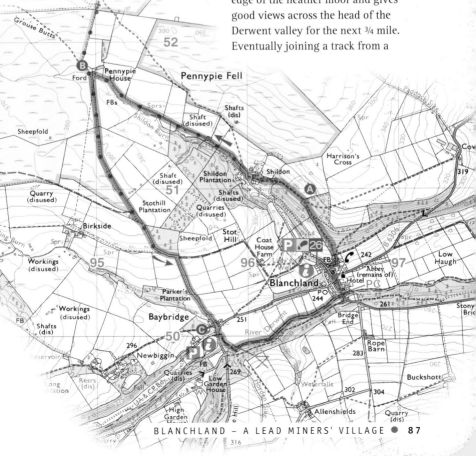

screened gas pumping station, leave the moor and follow a lane downhill beside a wood.

At the bottom, go right on the main lane past the Baybridge picnic area. Just before reaching a bridge across the River Derwent, abandon the lane for a footpath on the left signed to Blanchland and Carrick Ⓒ. A short length of duckboarding conducts you to the riverbank, where a very pretty path follows the crystal water as it babbles over a bouldery bed, overhung with trees. All too soon the path reaches Blanchland Bridge. Walk out to the lane and turn left back into the village. ●

The old mine engine house at Shildon

Ravenscar's alum works

Start
Robin Hood's Bay

Distance
9 miles (14.5km)

Height gain
1,400 feet (425m)

Approximate time
5 hours

Route terrain
Tracks, field and cliff paths

Parking
Station Car Park

OS maps
Landranger 94 (Whitby & Esk Dale), Explorer OL27 (North York Moors - Eastern area)

GPS waypoints
NZ 950 054
Ⓐ NZ 946 052
Ⓑ NZ 980 016
Ⓒ NZ 973 019
Ⓓ NZ 959 031
Ⓔ NZ 954 040

No one knows why the once isolated fishing village of Robin Hood's Bay and Bronze Age burial cairns on Brow Moor were associated with the legendary hero, but like Ravenscar, it was a haunt for smugglers. The completion of the coastal railway in 1885 turned Robin Hood's Bay into a popular resort, but entrepreneurial plans to revive Ravenscar, formerly a hive of industrial activity came to nought. While Robin Hood's beach is still popular, the picturesque railway line is now given over to walkers and cyclists and the abandoned alum quarries and works stand as an impressive relic of a once-important industry.

Leave the car park, heading past the former railway buildings along a narrow lane. At the bottom turn right, then after 100 yds at a bend, go left through a gate Ⓐ onto the old railbed. Winding at the edge of the high ground overlooking the vast sweep of Robin Hood's Bay, the track alternates between deep cuttings and high embankments that offer spectacular views along the coast. Farther on, it passes through disused quarries, where shale was dug for the manufacture of alum.

The railway The idea for the railway was first raised in 1848, but difficulties in determining a viable route and raising capital delayed its start and final completion. Largely a single line operation, steep gradients and the vagaries of coastal weather contributed to running difficulties and the 21-mile route between Scarborough and Whitby, stopping at eight intermediate stations, was never really profitable. However the popularity of seaside holidays brought something of a seasonal boom in the 1930s and camping cars were even introduced at several stations. The growth in car ownership after the last war finally sealed the line's fate and it was a victim of the Beeching cuts in 1965.

Approaching Ravenscar, the railway entered a short tunnel, but the path leaves just before that point, going through a gate to join a rising track. Follow it up to the right past the National Trust Coastal Centre to a road at the top Ⓑ.

Turn left in front of the hotel gates along a downhill track signed to Peak Fault, from which there is perhaps, the finest view of the walk. Below the hotel walls, the track bends sharply left above Raven Hall golf course, later curving right through scrubby woodland to join the Cleveland Way. A short distance

beyond, a path on the right **C** leads down to the site of the Peak alum factory.

Return to the main track and continue a little farther until the way is barred by a gate. Take a path on the right, which follows the field edge to the coast and carries on above the cliffs. After ¾ mile, the path emerges onto a lane **D**. Turn right down to a cottage, continuing past it along a descending stepped path to Stoupe Beck. *If the tide is safely out, you can walk the remainder of the way to Robin Hood's Bay along the rocky beach. Otherwise, carry on over a footbridge to climb energetically beyond.* Another short clifftop walk follows

The alum works

before the path once again falls sharply, this time emerging onto a lane above Boggle Hole **E**.

Turn right, but then almost immediately, double back left down to a bridge below the youth hostel. Walk past its front to begin another steep ascent to the top of the cliffs. You then have an easy walk across the fields before the coast path falls along a decked walkway towards Robin Hood's Bay. At the end, go down to the right to reach a small promenade above the

Mystery Prehistoric burials, a Roman signal station on the moors and tales of smugglers lend an air of intangible mystery, heightened by the story that Dr Francis Willis, physician to Europe's Royalty, quietly brought King George III here towards the end of the 18th century to treat him at Raven Hall for his 'madness'. Equally curious is Ravenscar itself. In 1895, led by John Septimus Bland and encouraged by the new railway, a consortium of Yorkshire businessmen planned a fashionable resort. Centred on a square by the station, they laid out streets and drains to serve some 1,200 houses and even gave the place a new name. But despite fine views, the windswept location and difficulty of reaching the beach damped the enthusiasm of potential purchasers and only a handful of houses were ever built.

beach, climbing a short flight of steps at its far end and then dropping to a slipway by the old lifeboat station, now a National Trust Information Centre. Turn left and follow the winding street up through the village to the car park at the top. ●

Alum A necessary chemical in tanning and dyeing as well as being used in the manufacture of candles and parchment, alum was discovered in the North Yorkshire shales, and Ravenscar was one of many places along the coast where it was dug. Quarrying began in 1640 and the clifftop factory was built to extract the salt. The process involved roasting the rock and dousing it with human urine, collected from towns up and down the coast and brought in by the boatload. The industry collapsed when an alternative process involving the treatment of colliery waste with sulphuric acid was discovered, and the works closed in 1862.

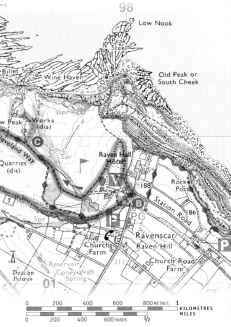

Further Information

 ## Walking Safety

Although the reasonably gentle countryside that is the subject of this book offers no real dangers to walkers at any time of the year, it is still advisable to take sensible precautions and follow certain well-tried guidelines.

Always take with you both warm and waterproof clothing and sufficient food and drink. Wear suitable footwear, such as strong walking boots or shoes that give a good grip over stony ground, on slippery slopes and in muddy conditions. Try to obtain a local weather forecast and bear it in mind before you start. Do not be afraid to abandon your proposed route and return to your starting point in the event of a sudden and unexpected deterioration in the weather.

All the walks described in this book will be safe to do, given due care and respect, even during the winter. Indeed, a crisp, fine winter day often provides perfect walking conditions, with firm ground underfoot and a clarity unique to this time of the year. The most difficult hazard likely to be encountered is mud, especially when walking along woodland and field paths, farm tracks and bridleways – the latter in particular can often get churned up by cyclists and horses. In summer, an additional difficulty may be narrow and overgrown paths, particularly along the edges of cultivated fields. Always ensure appropriate footwear is worn.

 ## Walkers and the Law

The Countryside and Rights of Way Act (CRoW Act 2000) extends the rights of access previously enjoyed by walkers in England and Wales. Implementation of these rights began on 19 September 2004. The Act amends existing legislation and for the first time provides access on foot to certain types of land – defined as mountain, moor, heath, down and registered common land.

Where You Can Go
Rights of Way

Prior to the introduction of the CRoW Act, walkers could only legally access the countryside along public rights of way. These are either 'footpaths' (for walkers only) or 'bridleways' (for walkers, riders on horseback and pedal cyclists). A third category called 'Byways open to all traffic' (BOATs), is used by motorised vehicles as well as those using non-mechanised transport. Mainly they are green lanes, farm and estate roads, although occasionally they will be found crossing mountainous area.

Rights of way are marked on Ordnance Survey maps. Look for the green broken lines on the Explorer maps, or the red dashed lines on Landranger maps.

The term 'right of way' means exactly what it says. It gives a right of passage over what, for the most part, is private land. Under pre-CRoW legislation walkers were required to keep to the line of the right of way and not stray onto land on either side. If you did inadvertently wander off the right of way, either because of faulty map reading or because the route was not clearly indicated on the ground, you were technically trespassing.

Local authorities have a legal obligation to ensure that rights of way are kept clear and free of obstruction, and are signposted where they leave metalled roads. The duty of local authorities to install signposts extends to the placing of signs along a path or way, but only where the authority considers it necessary to have a signpost or waymark to assist persons unfamiliar with the locality.

The New Access Rights
Access Land

As well as being able to walk on existing rights of way, under the new legislation you now have access to large areas of open land. You can of course continue to use rights of way footpaths to cross this land, but the main difference is that you can now

Countryside Access Charter

Your rights of way are:

- public footpaths – on foot only. Sometimes waymarked in yellow
- bridle-ways – on foot, horseback and pedal cycle. Sometimes waymarked in blue
- byways (usually old roads), most 'roads used as public paths' and, of course, public roads – all traffic has the right of way

Use maps, signs and waymarks to check rights of way. Ordnance Survey Explorer and Landranger maps show most public rights of way

On rights of way you can:

- take a pram, pushchair or wheelchair if practicable
- take a dog (on a lead or under close control)
- take a short route round an illegal obstruction or remove it sufficiently to get past

You have a right to go for recreation to:

- public parks and open spaces – on foot
- most commons near older towns and cities – on foot and sometimes on horseback
- private land where the owner has a formal agreement with the local authority

In addition you can use the following by local or established custom or consent, but ask for advice if you are unsure:

- many areas of open country, such as moorland, fell and coastal areas, especially those in the care of the National Trust, and some commons
- some woods and forests, especially those owned by the Forestry Commission
- country parks and picnic sites
- most beaches
- canal towpaths
- some private paths and tracks Consent sometimes extends to horse-riding and cycling

For your information:

- county councils and London boroughs maintain and record rights of way, and register commons
- obstructions, dangerous animals, harassment and misleading signs on rights of way are illegal and you should report them to the county council
- paths across fields can be ploughed, but must normally be reinstated within two weeks
- landowners can require you to leave land to which you have no right of access
- motor vehicles are normally permitted only on roads, byways and some 'roads used as public paths'

---

lawfully leave the path and wander at will, but only in areas designated as access land.

Where to Walk

Areas now covered by the new access rights – Access Land – are shown on Ordnance Survey Explorer maps bearing the access land symbol on the front cover.

'Access Land' is shown on Ordnance Survey maps by a light yellow tint surrounded by a pale orange border. New orange coloured 'i' symbols on the maps will show the location of permanent access information boards installed by the access authorities.

Restrictions

The right to walk on access land may lawfully be restricted by landowners, but whatever restrictions are put into place on access land they have no effect on existing rights of way, and you can continue to walk on them.

Dogs

Dogs can be taken on access land, but must be kept on leads of two metres or less between 1 March and 31 July, and at all times where they are near livestock. In addition landowners may impose a ban on all dogs from fields where lambing takes place for up to six weeks in any year. Dogs may be banned from moorland used for grouse shooting and breeding for up to five years.

General Obstructions

Obstructions can sometimes cause a problem on a walk and the most common of these is where the path across a field has been ploughed over. It is legal for a farmer to plough up a path provided that it is restored within two weeks. This does not always happen and you are faced with the dilemma of following the line of the path, even if this means treading on crops, or walking round the edge of the field. Although the latter course of action seems the most sensible, it does mean that you would be trespassing.

Other obstructions can vary from overhanging vegetation to wire fences across the path, locked gates or even a cattle feeder on the path.

Use common sense. If you can get round the obstruction without causing damage, do so. Otherwise only remove as much of the obstruction as is necessary to secure passage.

If the right of way is blocked and cannot be followed, there is a long-standing view that in such circumstances there is a right to deviate, but this cannot wholly be relied on. Although it is accepted in law that highways (and that includes rights of way) are for the public service, and if the usual track is impassable, it is for the general good that people should be entitled to pass into another line. However, this should not be taken as indicating a right to deviate whenever a way is impassable. If in doubt, retreat.

Report obstructions to the local authority and/or the Ramblers.

 ## Useful Organisations

Camping and Caravanning Club
Tel. 0845 130 7633
www.campingandcaravanningclub.co.uk

English Heritage
Tel. 0870 333 1181
www.english-heritage.org.uk

Forestry Commission
Tel. 0845 3673787
www.forestry.gov.uk

National Parks and AONBs:
Howardian Hills AONB
Tel. 0845 034 9495
www.howardianhills.org.uk

Nidderdale AONB
Tel. 01423 712950
www.nidderdaleaonb.org.uk

North Pennines AONB
Tel. 01388 528801
www.northpennines.org.uk

North York Moors National Park
Tel. 01439 770657
www.northyorkmoors.org.uk

Northumberland Coast AONB
Tel: 01665 511207
www.northumberlandcoastaonb.org

Northumberland National Park
Tel. 01434 605555
www.northumberland-national-park.org.uk

The National Trust
Membership and general enquiries
Tel. 0844 800 1895
www.nationaltrust.org.uk

Natural England
Tel. 0845 600 3078
www.naturalengland.org.uk

Ordnance Survey
Tel. 08456 050 505
www.ordnancesurvey.co.uk

Public Transport
Traveline
Tel. 0871 200 2233
www.traveline.org.uk

Tourist information
Enjoy England
www.enjoyengland.com

Youth Hostels Association
Tel. 0800 019 1700
www.yha.org.uk

Text: Dennis and Jan Kelsall
Photography: Dennis and Jan Kelsall, Brian Conduit
Editorial: Ark Creative (UK) Ltd
Design: Ark Creative (UK) Ltd

This product includes mapping data licensed from Ordnance Survey® with the permission of the Controller of Her Majesty's Stationery Office. © Crown Copyright 2011. All rights reserved. Licence number 150002047. Ordnance Survey, the OS symbol and Pathfinder are registered trademarks and Explorer, Landranger and Outdoor Leisure are trademarks of the Ordnance Survey, the national mapping agency of Great Britain.

ISBN: 978-1-85458-637-7

While every care has been taken to ensure the accuracy of the route directions, the publishers cannot accept responsibility for errors or omissions, or for changes in details given. The countryside is not static: hedges and fences can be removed, field boundaries can alter, footpaths can be rerouted and changes in ownership can result in the closure or diversion of some concessionary paths. Also, paths that are easy and pleasant for walking in fine conditions may become slippery, muddy and difficult in wet weather, while stepping stones across rivers and streams may become impassable.

If you find an inaccuracy in either the text or maps, please write to Crimson Publishing at the address below.

Printed in Singapore. 1/11

First published in Great Britain 2011 by Crimson Publishing, a division of:
Crimson Business Ltd,
Westminster House, Kew Road, Richmond, Surrey, TW9 2ND

www.totalwalking.co.uk

A catalogue record for this book is available from the British library.

Front cover: Byland Abbey
Page 1: Lindisfarne Priory

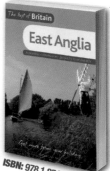

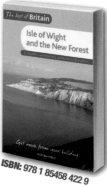
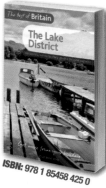